LLEGE

D0260666

Afternoon Raag

By the same author

A Strange and Sublime Address

Amit Chaudhuri

Afternoon Raag

HEINEMANN : LONDON

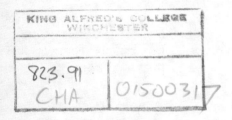
First published in Great Britain 1993
by William Heinemann Ltd
an imprint of Reed Consumer Books Ltd
Michelin House, 81 Fulham Road, London SW3 6RB
and Melbourne, Auckland, Singapore and Toronto

Reprinted 1993

A CIP catalogue record for this title
is available from the British Library
ISBN 0 434 12349 8

Printed in England by Clays Ltd, St Ives plc

Acknowledgements

I am grateful to the Authors' Foundation and the Kathleen Blundell Trust, administered by the Society of Authors, for grants that enabled me to complete this book, and to the editors of *New Writing 2*, where Chapter Four was first published.

Afternoon Raag

In memory of Pandit Govind Prasad Jaipurwale
(1941–1988)

The doorbell rings. The music-teacher comes in.
He is smiling as usual. His body is smiling. He is
                    humming a complicated tune –
outside, wind, light and rain revolve the landscape in a
                    shifting treadmill of shadow.
Inside, in the cool room, my mother and the music-
                    teacher sit on the carpet, as usual,
enclosed, in the drawing-room, by sofas and tables and
                    paintings and curios.

My mother plays the harmonium; she begins to sing.
Her fingers on the black and white keys make, of her
                    hand, a temple with many doors.
When the music-teacher joins in intermittently, he
              shows what a strange thing the human voice is,
this tiny instrument in the throat, with its hidden
            universe of notes, its delicate, inscrutable laws.
A raag, spacious as the mansion the rain builds,
              enfolds – and sighs, like one of the elements.
Inside the great architecture of the raag, through the
            clear archway of notes, world without humans,
two figures sit, each alone
– my mother and the music-teacher – enclosed by sofas
                    and paintings and curios.

The music teacher is listless today.
He does not respond.
My mother is just a little irritated as she sings, but she
      is afraid, too, of something she does not understand.
The music-teacher has merged with the sofa behind
          him, momentarily indistinguishable from the soft,
              indifferent contours of the furniture,

with the disturbing patience and resignation of
                                    furniture.
His wife, his widowed mother, his brother, his
                brother-in-law, his sister, his four children,
the jewelled constellation that appeared at his birth,
are moving away from him. He is alone, sitting on the
                    carpet, leaning his back against the sofa.
Behind this moment of serenity in this small, calm
                                            room,
with its clear, cool space flowing in and out of a
                                        listlessness,
is something liquid and grieving, something that
            cannot tolerate its own shimmering presence,
but melts away from itself all the time, like the giant
                walls of rain, or tears, or something else.

The music-teacher is dying.
He does not know it, but he will be dead in less than a
                                        year's time.
He will not see the rain again.
He does not know it. His ignorance of death surrounds
                him like a halo, an intimacy with God.
My mother does not know it.
The rain does not know it.
The world is being washed clean by the rain.
        Something in us, human but one with the season,
is also being washed clean, tear after tear, cloudburst
                                        in silence.

Nothing remains but the human voice, this tiny
                        instrument inside the throat
endeavouring to carry a world inside it. Then, that too
                                becomes silent.
The raag, self-created galaxy of notes, sigh of the
            elements, sighs like the rain, passes into nature.
We do not see him. My mother goes on singing, as if
            unaware. He moves further away, not drawing
                            attention to himself.
We do not see him now, except as a shadow against
                                        the sofa,
merged with the furniture, the endless meditation of
                                        furniture,
his lungs filled with water, his face and feet swollen
                        and his mouth smiling,

viii

become one with the reverie of furniture.
My mother sits there, singing, the rain falls, melting
                                    from its own presence,
the moment perfected not by art but by mortality, the
    mortal moment, repeating and repeating its own life.

One

Each year, in Oxford, new students come and old ones disappear; after a while, one knows the streets and by-lanes, all of which lead to each other, by heart; in the north, no one goes beyond Summertown, and the road leading to London goes out via Headington. On the first day of Michaelmas, men and women in black gowns walk to matriculation ceremonies, and at the end of the year they wear these gowns again, unhappily, to take exams; then, after the exams, the town is nearly empty, and the days, because of that peculiar English enchantment called Summer Time, last one hour longer; and Oxford, in the evening, resembles what an English town must have looked like in wartime, the small shops open but unfrequented, an endangered, dolorous, but perfectly vivid peace in the lanes, as the eye is both surprised by, and takes pleasure in, a couple linked arm in arm, or a young man conversing with a woman on a polished doorstep, and then the early goodbyes. It is like what I imagine a wartime township to have been, because all the young people, with their whistling, their pavement to pavement chatter, their beer-breathed, elbow-nudging polemics, are suddenly gone, leaving the persistent habits of an old way of life, the opening and shutting of shops, intact, a quiet, empty bastion of civilisation and citizenry. It is because of its smallness, repetition, and the evanescence of its populace, that Oxford is dream-like.

From the window of my room I could see a library and a faculty building, and a path, curving slightly, that led to a college. Students, dressed in the oddest of clothes, in secretive overcoats, in long and black primitive skirts, men with ear-rings, women wearing gypsy ornaments, would gather each morning for lectures, or pass in and out of doors recklessly with books clutched to their bosoms, or sit on the steps in abandonment, as if they had forgotten their appointments. The path, which is flanked by hedges that turn bright red in the autumn, I could see far into; at one point, it ran over a canal, so that I sensed water there. This intuition of water came to me again when I was visiting Worcester College; it was an unhappy day, because I was still vacillating between Mandira and Shehnaz, falling asleep by one woman at night and spending the day with the other, but I had, for a forced, lucid period of time, come here to attend a seminar on Lawrence. On entering the first quad, I saw that the light – it was evening – behind the wall at the end of the garden was different; as if the sun had set there, so that I imagined a seashore and a horizon. Later, I learnt that there was a lake there.

Dr Mason's room was simple, with two sofas, adjacent to each other, and a study table, next to which there was a chair on which he sat. It was a well-lighted and warm room, but its colours were cool – furniture browns and wallpaper purples and magnolias and greys, the colours that create, in afternoon light or evening shadow, the abidingness of an English interior. Three undergraduates, myself, and two other graduate students, sat on the sofa, while another undergraduate, bearded and with spectacles, placed himself on the window-sill and never said a word, but listened to the others' words, seeming to weigh them, and it was his silence that I deciphered for agreement or disapproval. Dr Mason was a polite, even kind, man, a very big man, not very old, facing us in his armchair. Some students had open copies of *The White Peacock* in their hands, and as we talked of Lawrence, extolled him, applauded him, and most invigoratingly of all, corrected him, it seemed both strange and natural to hear our own voices. The mind focused itself upon the sphere of the room and the table lamp, and then dilated vaguely and darkly into a consciousness of Lawrence-country, and then focused upon the room again, and this dilation and constriction went on for a long time, like breathing. An hour later, we got up to leave. There was laughter, and a relaxed certainty with which we let each other go, almost released each other, into the night. How unique student life is, with its different rooms, its temporary enclosures and crystallisations, its awareness and memory of furniture and windows and spaces.

Two

arly in the morning, light would frame the
curtains of my window, although at times
there was only a dull whiteness. When I
parted the curtains, I would look out into the
curving road to the next college, the closed doors
of the library, and the pavements. The wind
would make a piece of paper move, and, touching
the window, I would sense the cold outside. As I
am used to the sound of crows in the morning,
this absence of noise would fill me with a melan-
choly which was difficult to get rid of because it
seemed to have no immediate cause. It was only
when I saw students, with their odd, comical
gait, and their touchingly disguised sleepiness,
walking down that road, growing, little by little, in
number as the morning wore on, that I would feel
an at-homeness and pleasure in their rhythm. It
was around this time that Shehnaz too would set
out from her college and come down the same

road, indistinguishable from the other students, but with her own thoughtful gait, a backward-lookingness, happy in a simple way in having this opportunity to walk to her library in Broad Street, and devote a fresh day to copying out notes, stopping at my room for half an hour on her way there.

She was, essentially, a lonely person searching for the right company, a wise little girl in a woman's body, dressed in black trousers, a blue top and a coat, and black sneakers. Her hair was long and striking and untidy; solemnly, she carried a file full of papers under her arm, and a clumsy, oversized bag whose significance was that there was a tiny packet of Marlboro Lights in it. She had been married once, very briefly, and then divorced; later, she had an involvement in Oxford which came to nothing. It was towards the end of this involvement that I first met her, through a friend, and then we would exchange nods when we passed each other by on the bicycle-lined pavement of a street which led to a pub and a junction. Students, drolly crossing the street, or lavishly arguing, filled out the spaces in the street and the time between one meeting and the other upon this repeated route, so that the street, with its daily, inconsequential academic excitement and drama, has become indissoluble from the inner life of our early meetings, and Oxford, its climate and architecture, seems not so much a setting as a part of the heart of our friendship.

By the time she would get up to leave, the

rest of the building would have woken up and be moving about. Noises were transmitted through walls and doors; a radio; a knowing, crowded murmur in the kitchen; footsteps in the corridor; the main door shutting; the firm but almost non-physical sound of footsteps on the gravel; there were many lives in the building made transiently one by sound. I had a feeling of being surrounded, as on a ship or a train, by personal routines and habits that would not be known again, that had their natural place in some larger, more fixed habitat, and the morning noise had about it, there-fore, the concentratedness, the temporariness, and the pathos of the noise of shared travel. It was at this time, after the sun had risen, and lives, with-out apparent reason, once more began excitedly, when there was shouting upstairs, windows open-ing, last-minute preparations, and a joy akin to that felt by passengers approaching a port, that Shehnaz would get up to leave, listening, with one ear, to the voices of other students, smiling at what they were saying. Everything they said she found worth listening to, especially if she had had a happy morning with me; she had an uncanny sensitivity to the presence of people in small spaces, in corridors, in doorways, as others have to landscapes, or to places. Being there in that corridor at that moment, as students sheepishly came out of rooms and vanished into the kitchen or the toilet, was a real experience for her.

*

Sharma lived in another room in the same building. Sometimes, in the morning, he would come down in his shorts to have coffee with me. Banging on the door in a forthright manner, he would enter, and if I happened to be midway through practising a raag, he would sit quietly on a chair and nod and shake his head in vigorous appreciation as I sang. The irrepressible bodily meaning of the words 'to be moved', which we have come to associate with mental and aesthetic response, was apparent when one looked at him listening to music. Sometimes he would keep rhythm to the song, arbitrary temporal divisions that he slapped and pounded on the table, and when I had finished he would still be doing this, as if he could no longer stop. Later, he would walk around the room possessively, tapping the keys of my typewriter and reading aloud all the titles of the books on my shelf in order to make himself more conversant with the English language.

Once or twice, it happened that I had gone outside, leaving my door open, and then returned and closed it, thinking I was alone. But Sharma, in the meanwhile, had come and hidden himself in the clothes-closet, from which, at a given moment, he emerged explosively. Towards the beginning of our friendship, he had told me very seriously that I was to help him improve his English. He was writing a thesis on Indian philosophy, but he longed to be a stylist. I would, thus, recommend to him a book whose language had given me pleasure, and he would read aloud passages from

Mandelstam or Updike or Lawrence to me, either in the morning or at midnight, times at which I was sleepy, he reading sonorous lines in a loud and unstoppable voice, interrupting himself only to demand comments from me that were both fair and encouraging. His English had a strong, pure North Indian accent, so that he pronounced 'joy' a little bit like the French 'joie', and 'toilet' like 'twilit'. Yet this accent, I soon learnt, was never to be silenced completely; it was himself, and however he trained himself to imitate the sounds of English speech, 'toilet', when he pronounced it, would always have the faint but unmistakable and intimate and fortunate hint of 'twilit'. His sentence-constructions were curious, with missing articles and mixed-up pronouns, but he compensated for these with an excess of 'Thank yous' and 'Sorrys', two expressions gratuitous in Indian languages, and therefore, no doubt, of great and triumphant cultural importance to him. His reading practice in the mornings, executed with the single-mindedness of a child practising scales by thumping the keys, remains for me one of the most relaxing memories of Oxford; me lying on the bed and patiently listening, a time of rootedness and plenitude, even of equable solitude, for with Sharma one is always alone, listening to him. Mandelstam, read by Sharma, took on a different, unsuspected life, odd, cubist, harmlessly egotistical, and atmospheric.

Three

andira lived in a room in college. She had come to Oxford two years after me, and I first saw her in hall. She spoke English, I noticed, with a slight American accent, talked actively at the table, walked in what is called 'a brisk manner', and was surrounded by English friends. She was small and roundish, and a favourite with the porters and stewards, who would wink at her, or put an arm around her, and call her 'love' or 'dear', as the English do, and not take her very seriously. I did not like her, but, when I was bored, I would go to her room and drink a cup of tea. I gradually got over my tentativeness, and came to realise that a knock on her door would not be unwelcome, for she was always very hospitable in her disorganised way. The first five minutes would be spent in me settling down, after a preamble during which I decided where I should sit, on the armchair in a way that was both tortured and patient, and then open a bantering conversation with her *in medias res*; all this I took to be courtesy, but it made her uncomfortable, for I remember her as a compound of movement and aimless speed, putting the kettle on the boil, and then running down a flight of stairs to the kitchen for her carton of milk. Shyness made her quick, while I, by contrast, was slow. When she was gone for that minute, I would be alone in her room, with the photographs on the wall, the secret things and cups and clothes in her cupboard, the badly made bed, the washbasin and mirror, the textbooks on the table and the floor, absorbing the materiality of the room and also its cheerful, fleeting makeshiftness, and not knowing what to think. She was not a very tidy person, but her attempt at order and creating the semblance of a household, even the clumsy tear at the spout of the milk-carton, touched me. These undergraduate rooms were larger and more comfortable to look at than the box-like, modern rooms in my building. A light hung from the ceiling, enclosed by a comical, globe-like shade, and at evening it gave a light that was both encompassing and personal. The window opened on to a path to the garden and the hall, and all day, laughter and footsteps could be heard, coming and going, and these sounds too became a part of the room's presence.

In the morning, I looked forward to the small journey I made across the road, glancing right and left with avid interst for oncoming cars, to see if I had any mail. The pigeon-holes, after the poverty of Sunday, its forced spiritual calm, seemed to overflow humanely with letters on Monday, and even if I had not got any, that small walk did not lose its freshness and buoyancy, and a tiny and acute feeling of hope did not desert me in all my mornings. From about half past nine to ten, there was a hubbub as students stooped or stood on tip-toe to peep into pigeon-holes, and sorted and sifted letters, and the mail-room had an air of optimism, of being in touch with the universe, found nowhere else in Oxford. When there *were* letters for me – the cheap, blue Indian aerogrammes from my mother – they lay there innocently like gifts from a Santa Claus, they did not seem material at all, but magical, like signs. Then I would miss the special feeling of mornings at home, I would think benignly of my mother's good health, and how she suffers from nothing but constipation, how for three days she will go without having been to the toilet, with an abstracted look on her face, as if she were hatching an egg. Secretively, she will concoct a mixture of Isab-gol and water, and stir it ferociously before drinking it. Then, one day, like a revelation, it will come, and she will have vanished from human company. My father, a great generaliser, collector of proverbs, shows no concern over her health, displays no bitterness.

The furniture in Mandira's room – the bed, the study-table, its chair, the cupboard, the bookshelves – was old, enduring. The armchair was solid and stoic, and seemed to cradle the space that existed between its thick arms; one felt protected when one sat in it. As I got to know Mandira better, as we became intimate and then grew increasingly unhappy, the room became her refuge, her dwelling, and when she said, 'I want to go back to my room', the words 'my room' suggested the small but familiar vacuums that kept close around her, that attended to her and guided her in this faraway country. Because, for a foreigner and a student, the room one wakes and sleeps in becomes one's first friend, the only thing with which one establishes a relationship that is natural and unthinking, its air and light what one shares with one's thoughts, its deep, unambiguous space, whether in daytime, or in darkness when the light has been switched off, what gives one back to oneself. The bed and chairs in it had an inscape, a life, which made them particular, and not a general array of objects. That is why, when she spoke of her room, I think what she meant was the sense of not being deserted, of something, if not someone, waiting, of a silent but reliable expectancy.

The room had other rooms next to it and other rooms facing it. Sometimes, I would come up the staircase and enter the corridor to find Mandira leaning out of a half-closed door talking to the American girl who lived opposite, who would be standing by her own door. Even when I was inside the room, they would continue their conversation, and I would sit on the chair and watch Mandira's back; from there I could listen to

13

the voice of the invisible girl, and to her rising peals of laughter. For ten minutes they would say goodbye to each other, until there came a rounded silence, and Mandira closed the door. What was missing was the background sound of old people and children, of babies and mothers, of families; instead one heard people running up and down the staircase, or visitors approaching and knocking. There was a toilet near the room whose cistern gurgled candidly each time someone flushed it, and a bath to which men in dressing-gowns went solemnly in the evening, and women with towels around their heads, less solemn and with an air of freedom. From the bath everyone returned radiant and clean, and slightly ashamed. As I passed to or from Mandira's room, I would encounter them but not look at them, for I had learnt that the English do not consider it polite to look at each other, but nevertheless I remember the embarrassment of the men, and the opulent towels like Moorish turbans around the women's hair.

Four

Early mornings, my mother is about, drifting in her pale nightie, making herself a cup of tea in the kitchen. Water begins to boil in the kettle; it starts as a private, secluded sound, pure as rain, and grows to a steady, solipsistic bubbling. Not till she has had one cup of tea, so weak that it has a colour accidentally golden, can she begin her day. She is an insomniac. Her nights are wide-eyed and excited with worry. Even at three o'clock in the morning one might hear her eating a Marie biscuit in the kitchen. At such times, she moves gently as a mouse; we know it is her, and feel no danger. In the afternoons, she sleeps as a maidservant rubs cream on the soles of her feet. 'My feet are burning', she says. At the base of her ankle is a deep, ugly scar she got when a car ran over her foot when she was six years old. That was in a small town which is now in Bangladesh. Thus, even today, she hesitates superstitiously before crossing the road, and is painfully shy of walking distances. Her fears make her laughable. The scar is printed on her skin like a radiant star.

Her hair is troublesome and curly; when she was young, it was even thicker than it is now. It falls in long, black strands, but each strand has a gentle, complicated undulation travelling through it, like a mild electric shock or a thrill, that gives it a life of its own; it is visually analogous to a tremolo on a musical note. It is this tremolo that makes her hair curly and unmanageable and has caused her such lifelong displeasure. The easiest way she disposes of it is by gathering it compassionately into a humble, medium-sized bun, rendering it graceful with a final plastic hair-clip, or by thoughtfully metamorphosing it into a single serpent-like plait that looks paradoxically innocent. When the maidservant cleans the room and sweeps the dust to one corner, one may notice there, among other things, a few black strands with delicate, questioning curves that always float away with the merest breeze.

In the bedroom there is a weighing-machine with a flat, featureless face. Solemnly, in the morning, when my father is still asleep, my mother slips off her nightie, which weighs no more than a feather, and, quite naked, embarks upon the machine; for she will leave nothing to chance, let no extraneous factor prejudice its judicious needle. When she is satisfied with what she has seen, appalled or happy, she will alight on to earth again, and slip on her nightie. Then with short

16

steps (for she is no more than five feet and one and a half inches) she will cross all the way from the bedroom to the corridor to the hall to the veranda, making this long and lonely journey in the still hours of first light; there (on the veranda) she stands with the teacup balanced in one hand, pausing now and then in her thoughts (for she is always thinking) to sip her weak tea politely, watching the lane, in which Christian men in shorts are walking their Alsatians, with a genuine curiosity. Sometimes the famous music director, Naushad Ali, whose film songs we still hum in our solitary moments, can be seen walking down this lane with a cane in his hand and a companion by his side, his face wizened, almost Chinese, but humorous, gesticulating furiously with the hand that has waved at a thousand musical instruments, bringing a loud melody to life as he passes the sleepy lane. He is old now, in his eighties, and has suffered a few heart attacks. 'So he is still alive,' my mother thinks as she watches him. Meanwhile my father is sleeping in a most gentlemanly manner, taking care not to spill over into ungainly postures, his repose both stern and considerate as he lies on the bed with the quilt up to his chin.

After my father retired, we moved to this lane in the suburbs. Ours is the only apartment building in the lane; the rest are bungalows or cottages that belong to Christians. This is a Christian area; Portuguese names – Pedro, D'Silva and Gonsalves – twang in the air like plucked silvery guitar-strings. The Christian men are dark-complexioned and have maternal pot-bellies, because they like drinking. The women wear unfashionable dresses, flowery purple skirts that resemble old English wallpaper, exposing polished, maroon ankles and dark knees which they cover by pulling at the skirt-ends with chaste, dutiful fingers. These women and men eat pork, and sing and dance in cottages lit with cobwebs and dim bulbs, some of which have dates upon their facades (1923), and some of which are named after some beloved great-aunt (Helen Villa), no doubt a comical figure in her time. The Christians enjoy jokes and swear-words, and the women, when they are not sullen, are gently earthquaking with laughter at what John has just said with a straight face. They are in turn friendly, talking to you in queues at banks and post-offices, and short, taking offence when you innocently ask them for street-directions. Most of them are Roman Catholic; when asked, they pronounce themselves 'katlick', a word that sounds both childishly mischievous and appropriately rude.

When my mother finishes her tea, she walks to the harmonium which is resting in the hall upon a carpet, covered by a tranquil garment. But if it is not in the hall, she will ask Ponchoo, the cook, who is now awake, to bring it to the hall, and this he will do, holding it by the two metal rings on either side, anxious not to bump it against a door or a wall, transporting its heaviness with a pregnant woman's delicacy that dares not pause for breath, and with deep suspicion he will veer its precious body through the ins and outs of the corridor, and bending humbly, lay it in its place on the carpet. Then my mother will settle on the rug and unclip the bellows, pulling and pushing them with a mild aquatic motion with her left hand, the fingers of the right hand flowering upon the keys, the wedding-bangle suspended around her wrist. Each time the bellows are pushed, the round holes on the back open and close like eyes. Without the body music is not possible; it provides the hollow space for resonance as does the curved wooden box of the violin or the round urn of the sitar. At the moment of singing, breath tips in the swelling diaphragm as water does in a pitcher. The voice-box itself is a microscopic harp, its cords tautening and relaxing with each inflection. My mother begins to practise scales in the raag Todi.

Morning passes. When my father used to work in the city, and we lived in a flat in Malabar Hill overlooking the Arabian Sea, my mother would sometimes go to the Bombay Gymkhana in the afternoon and settle upon one of its spacious, boat-like wicker sofas, sinking into its oceanic cushions and dozing off till my father arrived for tea. Coming back from school, which was nearby, I would see her there as a silent composition of loved details; the deliberate, floral creases of her sari, the pale orange-brown glow of her skin, the mild ember-darkening of her lipsticked mouth, the patient, round fruition of her bun of hair, and the irrelevant red dot on her forehead. Seeing her was like roaming alone in a familiar garden. In cool, strategic corners, waiters stood in coloured waist-coats with numbered badges pinned to them; never did a name seem more apposite than then, in the afternoon, before people started coming in, when these waiters impassionedly *waited*, dark Goan men in neat clothes, inhaling and exhaling and lightly chattering among themselves. The most invigorating fact about the club was its long corridor, an avenue of light reflected off a polished floor and protected by arches. It was frequented mainly by company executives: general managers and directors. Dressed alike in tie and white pin-striped shirt and dark suit, they looked to me like angels. In the club, these managers would sit on chairs and childishly ring little brass bells to summon the waiters. With the waiters they shared a marital relationship of trust and suspicion, and an order wrongly taken could precipitate a storm and a crisis, a sudden display of emotions, shouts and insults. Food was in abundance, from the American hamburger to chop-suey to the local bhelpuri with its subversive smells of the narrow, spice-selling streets of west Bombay. My mother was always much amused by the sight of people eating around her, moving their mouths in a slow, moral way; human beings are the only creatures, she says, who eat habitually without hunger. Long-nosed Parsi lawyers stabbed their food, using knives and forks with jurisprudential ele-gance. Gujerati businessmen, educated in the school of life, employed fingers, holding the crispy wafer of the bhelpuri and biting it competitively, as if they were afraid it might bite them first.

Though we live now in the suburbs, habit still drives us to the city, from where my parents return at evening. My father falls asleep in the backseat of the Ambassador, this car which is now ours after his retirement, and my mother too dozes upon his shoulder. In a place near the rear-window are laid out the day's shopping, curved, inanimate objects my mother loves, such as spatulas and spoons, and little oases of food. The Ambassador is a spacious, box-like vehicle with a Taurean single-mindedness and a rickshaw's tenacity. It is known as a 'family car'; on Sundays, cousins and aunts on outings will sit, perspiring, inside it; I myself associate its hot floorboards, its aching gear-pulley, its recalcitrant pedals, with domesticity and the social events of childhood. Of all cars I know, it has perhaps the most uplifting name, as if its appointed office were to, wide-eyed, bring good news to the world. Meanwhile, our Ambassador joins the long, mournful crocodile of cars from Churchgate to Linking Road, and we know we are near home when we come to the Mahim Creek, where fishermen's boats are parked upon the sand; here, even if your eyes should be closed, or if you should be entering the city from the direction of the airport, you will be woken by the smell of dried or rotting fish, a strong but pure odour blown inland, bitter and sharply intimate as the scent of a woman's sex.

When it is evening in the lane, my parents

go down and walk for half an hour. Their lonely parade, their quiet ambitiousness as they walk up and down the compound, sometimes conferring, is witnessed by a watchman in khaki, sitting on a steel chair beneath blue light. This is an exercise they have rediscovered from when my father was a student in London, and my mother his newly-married wife, introverted, with a red dot on her forehead and vermilion in the parting of her hair, awkward but warm in her huge green overcoat. Then, too, they would walk together the wet roads from Belsize Park to Swiss Cottage. Afterwards, they go upstairs, and my mother sits on the bed, reading *The Afternoon Despatch and Courier*. She turns first to the last page, where Busybee's 'Round and About' is printed. Thus she continues this daily column about Bombay, its Irani restaurants, its post-offices, its buses, its cuisine, and this man's fictional wife and his dog. Years ago, my mother and I fell in love with Busybee's voice, its calm, even tone, and a smile which was always audible in the language. My father, meanwhile, is clipping his nails fastidiously, letting them fall on to an old, spread-out copy of the *Times of India*, till he sneezes explosively, as he customarily does, sending the crescent-shaped nail-clippings flying into the universe.

Five

The first few weeks I knew Shehnaz, when we were still getting to be friends, was an uncomplicated time. We made appointments and did not keep them; we made appointments to discuss when we might meet; we liked each other but were occupied, like children, with other things to do. Sometimes I am nostalgic for that make-believe busyness, full of innocence, of having 'other things to do', the prelapsarian background of lectures, bookshops, friends, our lives spent generously and routinely like rain-showers, stopping and starting again.

We decided to meet at the St Giles' Café near the Oxfam Bookshop. 'Do you know where it is?' she asked me with a smile; these sociable questions she would invest with a mischievousness, so that they became funny and meaningful, and I would always pretend to be embarrassed answering them. I did know the St Giles' Cafe; it was the only place in Oxford that served a strong and dark coffee, with a scorched South Indian flavour; a white froth, almost a scum, formed on the top even before they had put the milk in it. Unlike the coffee in the Middle and Senior Common Rooms, it was hot, and one could, with a certain satisfaction, admire the steam rising from the cup before one drank from it. The cafe was a small, ugly and crowded place, full of students, and tramps minding their own business, hatted and bearded, with an unworldly look about them, like musicians. On either side of each table, there was a bench, and one had to squeeze past people to sit down, or have people squeeze past you as they got out. Thus, as one made small adjustments in position, one was always feeling grateful or obliged, strangely powerful or powerless; one shrank and hunched, and then graciously expanded again, in regular accordion-like time. Each table also had an introvert who sat in the corner throughout and looked at no one. When people were called to take their food from the counter, they were not addressed by their names, but by their orders – 'Ham and eggs!' 'Plate of chips!' 'Bacon sandwich!' – and, calmly and without confusion, those who had been labelled so uniquely rose and walked towards the counter. Whenever the door opened, a draught entered from outside, but the baked air inside, smelling of frying bacon, cushioned us from the cold and from other influences. The paradoxical confluence of timelessness and movement in the cafe made it an ideal place for a first meeting between two foreign students.

Yet that meeting, comically, was not to be. It was the beginning of summer, and some girls walked barefoot that day on Cornmarket Street. There was a hustle and bustle, a festive hurry, and even Ryman's, the stationery shop, had inspired-looking customers queueing up to pay for envelopes and sheets of paper and sellotape. Sharma and I were roaming around at our ease in loose shirts, two Indians who might never have met in India, feeling at home, giving studious attention, as if it truly mattered, to shop-windows and an ancient organ-grinder, edging our way towards Westgate, both of us feeling boyish, and I especially younger because I was wearing sandals. It began to thunder then, and rain very hard, as it does at home; girls screamed in English, and people who were waiting for the bus panicked, but soon the crowds deployed themselves into neat and dripping little squadrons, cheerful and brave, and the entrance of the Clarendon Centre and the great department stores were converted into shelters with an unfussy swiftness. I had never seen it rain like this in England before; water collected in the lanes and flowed past us as it does in Calcutta; and the English were excited at first and then reasonable and collected, telling each other jokes and enjoying themselves; it was all a little like but yet very unlike the wise dailiness with which an Indian outwaits a shower. Sharma looked at the sky and felt poetic and told me how he was reminded of his village. Thus I did not meet Shehnaz that afternoon but waited outside a shop that sold shoes and saw wet and laughing people running and disappearing, and committed to memory the rare, leisurely couple who walked by, contented and soaked. Later, Shehnaz told me how she had cycled to the St Giles' Café after it had stopped raining, but had found it empty except for its owners, the stentorian callers of 'Ham and cheese' and 'Bacon sandwich', who were silent now, and busy mopping up the wet floors.

Six

Sohanlal comes in the mornings. He is married to my music-teacher's sister. Though he is quite short, he wears bright kurtas that come down below his knees. He demands the tablas from Ponchoo, strutting around the hall like a rooster in his early morning plumage. Then he tunes the smaller tabla with a hammer, and the bigger one on the left he booms with his fingertips. When he plays as my mother sings, his hands, which are old now, produce a pitter-patter noise. After twenty minutes, he takes a break, smoking a beedi on the veranda; and then, before he is finished, throws it away and coughs a dramatic smoker's cough. He likes doing things; returning, he takes out his handkerchief and dusts the harmonium, wiping the smooth, rectangular top. It is a harmonium made in Calcutta by Pakrashi, and he takes care to probe, his forefinger shrouded with the handkerchief, each English letter of PAKRASHI carved largely on the wood, blowing sensuously on the angular K and tracing the curves of the P and the R till he is satisfied. Then he polishes the black and white keys, and opens the cover; inside, the two rows of innumerable reeds lie bone-white, each reed a delicate white splinter, with a pinhead on one end and a flat metal strip on the belly. Sohanlal blows quietly upon them, as if they were on fire; how silent music is as it rests in these reeds, white paper-thin wands! He replaces the cover, because it is almost unpleasant to watch, the inner nakedness of a harmonium. Eagerly, he moves about again, his spacious pyjamas billowing around him. As he prepares to sit, they open at the bottom like alligator-mouths that have swallowed up his legs. After an hour, he glances at his wristwatch and collects his money politely and hurries out of the front door. Then next morning he is reincarnated in his fantastic kurta and pyjamas as if from a magic lamp.

It was on an afternoon in August I bought my first tanpura. We were visiting Calcutta then, and my music-teacher, my guru, had come with us and was living in our house; he was going to sing at a 'conference'. He would practise in the mornings, and take time off to vanish to the Kali temple, returning with a tilak, a great vermilion stain on his forehead, telling my mother 'Didi, I went to see Ma Kali!' On some mornings we would sing raag Bhairav together, our two voices and styles mingling closely and floating over the other sounds of the house – pigeons, and the distracted noise of servants – his voice sometimes carrying my hesitant voice, and negotiating the pathways of the raag, as a boat carries a bewildered passenger. In the moments of simple imbibing, I would forget my voice was my own and become an echo of his style and artistry. The greater part of the unfolding of a raag consists of a slow, evasive introduction in which the notes are related to each other by curving glissandoes, or meends. The straight, angular notes of Western music, composed and then rendered, are like print upon a page; in contrast, the curving meends of the raag are like longhand writing drawn upon the air. Each singer has his own impermanent longhand with its own arching, idiosyncratic beauties, its own repetitive, serpentine letters. With the end of the recital, this longhand, which, in its unravelling, is a matter of constant erasures and rewritings, is erased completely, unlike the notes of Western music, which remain printed upon the page.

That afternoon, we took the car to Rashbehari Avenue. My guru was dressed as usual in a loose white kurta and pyjamas. It must have been six or seven years before his death, and he must have just turned forty. He was humming a complicated tune with tiny embellishments when he was not talking to me, and the oil he had put in his hair before he combed it smelled sweet. We walked to the shop, no bigger than a room, called Hemen and Co. Outside, the pavement was broken, its edges blue-grey with ash from charcoal stoves; mosquitoes hung in the air. Ascending the three steps, we saw unfinished tanpuras and sitars, long patient necks and the comical but gracefully distended round urns; some instruments hung upside down from the ceiling like bats; and a man was planing a piece of wood. My tanpura was ready with its four new strings; I remember the tentative shyness with which I touched it.

Later, we sat on the floor in my room, and my guru taught me to tune the instrument. The tanpura can be held vertically on the lap or next to the upraised knee as it is played, when it looks male and perpendicular, or laid horizontally on the ground before one, when, with the surrendering slope of its long neck and the stable fullness of its urn, its mixture of acquiescence and poise, it looks feminine. The four strings provide only two notes as a background to the song; *sa*, or *shadja*, the first, the mother-note, from which all other notes come, with which one's relationship is permanent and unambiguous, and the second note, depending on the raag, the father-note, circumstantial but constructive. To tune the tanpura, you must turn the keys on its upper end, keys which are huge, ornate, and antique, like the doorknobs of a palace. On the nether end, upon the urn, there is a flat bridge on which the strings rest briefly, before they pass through small ivory-coloured beads that are used for the finer adjustments in tuning, and travel at last to a small plank of wood at the end, where, pierced through four open but infinitesimal eyes, they are knotted. While this painful business, this struggle, of tuning continues, four white threads are slipped beneath the strings as they lie on the bridge, and moved up and down till a point is discovered where each string loses its flat metallic note, and buzzes, a hum like that of the wandering drone, or electricity. This buzzing of the strings, this resonance, the musicians call *juwari*. That afternoon, my guru and I, like patient surgeons, tuned the tanpura till the room filled with notes *shadja* and *nikhad*.

When one remembers a scene from the past in which one is with a loved one who is now dead, it is not like a memory at all, but like a dream one is having before his death, a premonition. In this dream which precedes death, the person is tranquil and happy, and yet, without reason, you know he is to die. When we recall the dead, the past becomes a dream we are dreaming foretelling death, though in our waking moments we cannot properly interpret it or give it significance. My memory of the day I bought the tanpura with my guru is like such a dream.

Seven

Before I met Shehnaz, I led a domestic life
with Sharma, a warm kitchen-life of teas
and conversations. In this country where
afternoon comes suddenly, he was a desired and
happy interference, sewing my buttons, cooking
daal for dinner, advising me on which clothes to
wear, forcing me to buy new ones. What brought
us together, among other things, was a common
love for the English language. Each night, till
midnight, he would recount with delight new
idioms and words he had picked up during the
day, and from these words he would become
inseparable for about a week, using them in every
context, just as a child who has been given a gift
of new shoes spends a euphoric period wearing
them everywhere. After lunch, we would sometimes watch black and white British films from the
fifties on Channel Four, and Sharma would tell me
how charming he found the rhythms and accents

of Old English. He was a glum reader and connoisseur of dictionaries, an admirer of the *Collins'* and a baleful critic of the *OED*, and he had a special but clear-eyed insight into their limitations.

Eight

In Oxford, I would walk almost everywhere, because I had an inexplicable pride that prevented me from using buses. There were two kinds of local buses, the red double-decker and the small toy-like white and blue bus. When the double-deckers passed by, they looked grand and somehow inaccessible, while the white buses seemed warm and busy, with the people sitting in them clearly visible through the large windows. But sitting inside a bus was a different experience, unrelated to what one might have surmised from the outside. Once, I took a double-decker to Cowley Road. It was like entering another life, right from ascending the wide berth of the footboard at the entrance, clutching with great immediacy the pole-vaulter's pole that rose there from the floor, ignoring the stealthy staircase that crept primitively upward, to make one's way shyly inside, braving the curious but not unwelcoming

34

glances of other people. As the scene changed from the civic architecture of High Street to the grey brick houses and Indian restaurants on Cowley Road, bodies circulated gently and continually inside, as people got in and got out; it was strangely but peacefully crowded, and one had to cling economically to a loop of leather or a horizontal rod travelling over one's head, and sway containedly from the top of one's head to the base of one's feet, and privately regain one's balance, as the bus went on its stately but mildly drunken, intemperate course. Another time, I took a less dramatic journey on a white bus to Summertown. Everything about it was small and detailed, from the coin handed for my fare to the driver, the neat black seats, the roof lowering over my head. Behind me sat a group of chattering boys and girls, and their impudent London accent filled the bus. Only a little way away from me sat the Indian bus driver in his blue uniform, but for some reason I thought of him as 'Asian', and he became for me mysterious and unclassifiable. At each stop, he greeted kindly old ladies in a hearty English manner, 'Hullo, dear! It's lovely day, innit?' and later bid them inimitable farewells, 'Have a nice day, dear!', but the way he was more English than the English was very Indian, and there was something surprising about his utterances.

Cowley Road was on the other side, East Oxford. Long ago I had accompanied Sharma in hope of seeing an erotic Japanese film, *The Realm of the Senses*, to the Penultimate Picture Palace.

After the roundabout, three roads ran parallel to each other – St Clement's, Cowley Road, and Iffley Road. Full of spirit, we took the Cowley Road to the Picture Palace, but found, alas, that there were no tickets. The road was lined with Bangladeshi shops, and energetic little Muslim boys wearing skull-caps played on the pavement; they did not look foreign, but very provincial and East London. After darkness fell, the shops remained lighted and open, and old Pakistani gentlemen in overcoats, holding crumpled carrier-bags in their hands, had a chance to meet each other inside and converse in idiomatic Punjabi. Politics was discussed; the Bhuttos; Kashmir; cowardly India; bullying India; and the Indian cricket team was dismissed, quite rightly, with a contemptuous but decorous burst of air from the lungs. 'Asian' couples with shopping-trolleys went down aisles stacked with boxes of chilli powder, packets of dried fruit, jars of pickles, and imported vegetables – roots and tubers – with the flecked soil of Bangladesh still upon them; the shopkeeper continued his conversation in full-throated asides while his hands worked at the till; and to pay him, finally, in pounds rather than in rupees was like a joke whose meaning we both shared. There was a row of Indian restaurants along the road; at six o'clock, Muslim waiters stood significantly by the windows, and at night, the interiors glowed with a lurid red light. The furniture, selected with some tender and innocent idea of opulence in mind, was cheap and striking; honest Englishmen sat being

served among fluted armrests and large, menda-
cious pictures of palm-trees and winding rivers,
helplessly surrendering to an inexhaustible trickle
of eastern courtesy; everything, including the waiters, smelled strongly of mint and fenugreek. The
restaurants were seedy, but generous with life;
and from the silvery letters of the sign outside, to
the decor within, was a version of that style called
the 'oriental'.

Nine

It was in a small geometrical graduate room, in a modern building full of other such rooms, that I lived in those days. I was on the ground floor, and could hear the doorbell clearly when it rang. It used to make me, and perhaps every other student, specially alert and anticipatory; there would be a brief heightening and then a return to normalcy. In my pocket I carried, whenever I went out, two Yale doorkeys that gave me access to the building and my own door. Each was a twin of the other, unpretentious, golden-coloured, and dignified in the way it did not draw attention to the touch; one used the keys unconsciously and trustingly after the initial uncertain period of not knowing which was for which door was over. To my door was screwed a simple hook, from which my sweater and jacket, and later, in winter, my overcoat and scarf also, hung in a warm and voluminous pile. I did not notice until much later that all the hooks in Oxford, whether in public libraries or in college rooms, were the same as the one on my door, and belonged to a great family. There were two modern, comfortable armchairs opposite my bed, but in one of them the cords supporting the seat were a little loose, so that, when one sat on it, one slipped backward suddenly; then, after having spent one immobile and astonished moment in that position, one smiled and righted oneself. Even the good armchair was tilted at a slight, but more natural, axis, and I sat in it whenever I was tired, or had company. The armchairs, with their flat, sedentary cushions, were designed for society, but the bed was made for solitude. It had a straitened and measured narrowness, an austere frame made to contain the curves of a single body, to circumscribe it, carry it, give it a place, and when I slept at night, I possessed it entirely.

Ten

The loneliest of occupations was taking arm-loads of dirty clothing, stuffing them in a traveller's shoulder bag, and walking with it to the laundry room across the road. My main ambition was to diminish each moment, to hold as much as possible in as little space, to do things with the least depletion to time and effort. I disliked portioning out the load, for instance; I crammed in more than the bag could contain, and when, finally, I could not zip it, I would push against the clothes with all my weight, repeatedly and brutally, till they had been perfectly packed in.

Or I sat in my room with Lawrence's *Complete Poems* on my lap, looking at a page on which the long Laurentian lines spilled and overflowed from one verse to the other. I hated libraries, where human beings hunched strangely over their books, behaving like birds who were not eating, but studying, their prey, in a silence where the only things that whispered were the leaves of the books. Who were these people; what did they do at night; what peculiarly displaced lust drove them to fill in order-forms and push them confidentially towards a woman, and have a conveyor belt with a cargo of books turn endlessly in the basement for their benefit? I stayed safely in my room and tried to make sense of the beauty of 'Bavarian gentians, big and dark, only dark,/ darkening the day-time', or 'Have you built your ship of death, O have you?', or 'the fragile ship of courage, the ark of faith/ with its store of food and little cooking pans', or, especially, 'You tell me I am wrong./ Who are you, who is anybody to tell me I am wrong?', while the sound of someone making coffee entered my reading, and a portrait of Lawrence, gaunt, red-bearded, stared at me like a demon and kept me company.

I rented a television set for a few months, and became acquainted with Postman Pat and Blue Peter, and my afternoons were shaped by a soothing jumble of quiz-shows, word-games, and 'Fifteen to One'. Though poor in general knowledge, at guessing synonyms, and at making sense of the teasing, child-like nuisance of letters in an anagram, my mind, for a while, joyously deluded itself that it was in a state of agile and athletic excitement, and loved nothing more than being vanquished, in the end, by a retired widow from Dorset or a stuttering unemployed electrician from Leicester, sweet and harmless-looking people who had nevertheless used their empty hours to squeeze from themselves a razor-sharp competence in these matters.

There were times when I escaped to London, and as people fell asleep on the coach, their heads nodding and chiming in unison, I had occasion to think of my parents speaking to each other in Sylheti, or the sensation of standing on a veranda on a hot day. Scenes flashed past; and they flashed past when I returned in the evening, when I would see miles of suburbia on the edge of the motorway, house after house with a fragile, liminal television aerial on the roof, beneath a sky from which birds and clouds fast disappeared. It seemed that if extra-terrestrial intelligence had a message for earth, it would be here, among these nondescript houses, at this moment, as it darkened outside and a family gathered around a television, that they would send it, to be recognised and deciphered by, of course, a boy in shorts with dreams in his head.

Eleven

T wo sisters, Chhaya and Maya, take turns to clean the bathroom in our house in Bombay. I have seen the younger one, Chhaya, a girl with two protruding teeth who leaned wistfully between chores against a door to listen to my mother practise, or ran to snatch the bag of rubbish from Ponchoo, grow to a young woman with kaajal around her eyes, and unexpected breasts, two small, painless swellings. On the festival of Raakhi, she ties a thread around my wrist with a crazy silver flower upon it. Maya, the older one, is silent, ebony-dark, and wears clothes made from a shimmering synthetic material with silvery or purple hues, so that, even while collecting rubbish, she looks minty and refreshing.

The bathroom has a large square mirror like a window into which my father looks in the mornings. He wears floppy, unsmart pyjama trousers with buttons on the front which often remain inadvertently open, creating a dark, tiny fairytale entrance. After shaving, he splashes Old Spice on his cheeks, and the skin begins to glow with a faint green light. His hair started to grey when he was thirty, so he dyes it an unrealistic black, leaving one white plume smoking above his forehead. In the flat in Malabar Hill, where there was a bathtub, I used to hear him all my childhood rubbing the soles of his feet on it while bathing, making a sombre but musical sound as that of a double-bass.

In my childhood, too, my mother's enormous friend, Chitrakaki, would visit us in the afternoons. This was when we lived in a flat in a tall building overlooking the sea, the Marine Drive, and the horizon. Together they would nap, my mother's feet hidden by a cotton sheet, Chitrakaki, all two hundred pounds of her, inhabiting a loose, long gown and snoring and shuddering malarially in her sleep, both of them suspended a hundred feet above the earth without knowing it. Beneath them the Arabian Sea rushed and the earth moved, while their heads rested on pillows so soft that they were like bodies of pure flesh without skeleton. Bai, the maidservant, while she sat on the floor and rubbed oil upon my mother's burning toes, and I, sitting beside her and looking over the edge of the bed, admired the trembling and lack of composure of Chitrakaki's body, as her stomach soared and climbed and then toppled over, her head, though it was perfectly still, seeming to move animatedly behind her stomach. If Bai and I smiled at each other and passed satirical comments between her snores, she would say, in a god-like voice, 'I can hear everything.' She is now dead, though I remember her as before, waking from that sleep with my mother, and drinking tea, and avariciously cupping a spiced mixture of peanuts and thin crispy strands of gramflour that looked like screws or nails, and chewing upon it with an ostrich-like satisfaction in strange things. For, truly, both she and my mother loved this edible scrap, this tea-time assortment of spiced nuts and bolts; sometimes, she would bring with her a box of chakli, a savoury that is hard and brown and runs round itself in gnarled, concentric circles, and is like a coral, or the body of a sea-horse. Once or twice, we even went to a South Indian café together, for Chitrakaki loved exploring the tastes of different regions. Here, we ate from polished formica tables, and were served by dignified Tamil waiters who, dressed in an impeccable uniform, looked like the soldiers of an ancient army. These men emerged from hot, swinging kitchen doors with plates balanced upon their palms, and on the plates were huge 'paper' dosas. These are large white cylinders made of rice paste; from a distance, they look like rolled-up rugs, and coming closer, they resemble ridiculous headdresses of vast importance; from table to table, the waiters bore them glumly, as if they were gifts.

When I think of food, I think of the cat-like way my mother disposes of fish-bones, and eats the head of the rohu fish, meticulously destroying its labyrinths. Here a silent contest ensues, as she chews and bites at it from all sides, till the head disappears and the indigestible bones lie clean and polished on one corner of the plate. At dinner, our leftovers – chicken bones, ribs, the white comb-like tail of the pomfret, which is simple and symmetrical – we deposit upon her beggar's plate for her to chew and gnash and then blissfully spit out. My father, the most serious person at the table, uses, unexpectedly, a fork and a spoon to eat. He cannot begin till he has been served, and till that moment, remains sombre and paralysed. Once started, he floods his plate with daal, till it has made a yellow lake with white hillocks of rice upon its banks.

Twelve

In the afternoon, Mohan, my music-teacher's brother, and Sohanlal, his brother-in-law, ring the doorbell. Ponchoo then silently brings out the tablas and tuning-hammer from the cupboard, and the big tabla, shaped like half a globe, he balances between one arm and his chin maternally; the smaller one he clutches lightly but firmly by the strong cords of bark along its sides. Mohan and Sohanlal take a long time settling down, talking in their own language, the latter chattering very fast, while Mohan, a man of few words, sits carefully on the sofa. It is easy to see that Mohan is related to my music-teacher, that he is his brother, because their faces are similar, especially the colour of their skin, Mohan perhaps even a little darker than my music-teacher was. The timbre of Mohan's voice is also like my guru's, slightly husky, not loud or deep. Though he may not be aware of it, it is impossible for others not to see my guru come to life, in flashes, in Mohan's facial expressions, his turns of phrase, and his gestures. But Mohan is an unassuming man, while my guru, shorter and a little plump, was a show-off, doing astonishing feats with his voice and then chuckling gleefully at our admiration. Laughter is drawn out reluctantly from Mohan, who I think used to both hero-worship and self-effacingly humour his brother (he told me once he had turned to tabla-playing because there couldn't be two singers in a family, and that, when they were both learning the intricacies of vocal music from their father, he found his elder brother much too quick, much too clever to compete with), while my guru, especially when singing, would laugh happily after a difficult taan, and shake with mirth when he arrived at, after much deliberately drunken meandering, the sama, bringing a small, reluctant smile to his younger brother's lips. On tapes on which I recorded my guru singing in my house, complex melodic leaps and falls performed by him can be heard punctuated by brief chuckles.

When a singer performs, it is the job of the accompanists to support him dutifully and unobtrusively. A cyclical rhythm-pattern – say, of sixteen beats – is played at an unchanging tempo on the tabla, and the song and its syllables are set to this pattern, so that one privileged word in the poem will coincide ineluctably with the first of the sixteen beats in the cycle. This first beat is called the sama, and much drama, apprehension, and triumph surround it. For the singer is allowed to, even expected to, adventurously embark on rhythmic voyages of his own, only to arrive, with sudden, instinctive, and logical grace, once more at the sama, taking the audience, who are keeping time, unawares. Once this is achieved, the logic seems at first a flash of genius, and then cunningly pre-meditated. While the pretence is kept up, and the singer's rhythm appears to have lost itself, the tabla-player, with emotionless sobriety, maintains the stern tempo and cycle, until the singer, like an irresponsible but prodigious child, decides to dance in perfect steps back into it. Similarly, when a singer is executing his difficult melodic patterns, the harmonium-player must reproduce the notes without distracting him. The tabla and harmonium players behave like palanquin-bearers carrying a precious burden, or like solemn but indulgent guardians who walk a little distance behind a precocious child as it does astonishing things, seeing, with a corner of their eye, that it does not get hurt, or like deferential ministers clearing a path for their picturesque prince, or like anonymous and selfless spouses who give of themselves for the sake of a husband. Mohan, who plays the tabla with clarity and restraint, created the ground on which my guru constructed his music, and Sohanlal, attentively playing the harmonium, filled in the background. In the care of these two custodians, my guru sang and shone with his true worth.

Thirteen

Chhaya and Maya would spend the morning sweeping and cleaning and collecting rubbish. Their mother, a towering, mild woman, cleaned the stairs; sometimes, her husband, that pudgy, well-behaved man in khaki shorts, stood in for her, loitering in the compound, decoratively wielding a jhadu. This small family, father, mother, and two daughters, was employed by the Building Society. What they did with the implements of their trade – bucket, rag, water, disinfectant, jhadu, broom – was a mystery. A combination of these things did not automatically add up to cleanliness. From eight to twelve, one or the other of the sisters, bucket in one hand, jhadu in the other, made an independent, breezy tour of each flat in the seven-storeyed building.

Chhaya was the younger one, plump, extrovert, with dimples and protruding teeth. She did no work, but was on good terms with everyone.

From time to time, my mother preached to her to study hard and educate herself at the municipal school she never seemed to attend. She was interested neither in work, nor in studies, nor in looking pretty. The things she was interested in were my mother's singing practice in the morning, and when I would get married. Her older sister, in contrast, was a sensitive, overweight, round-faced girl who was exceptionally dark; she suffered because of this, and worked silently, almost sullenly. She never smiled, even by mistake; she seemed to think it would make her look ridiculous. By remaining silent, she tried not to draw attention to herself, but her very uncomfortableness made one notice her. The few times I caught her eye, she did not look, but glowered, at me. Then, a few years later, after she had passed puberty, she lost weight and gained a figure. Small, dark, and round-faced, she looked pretty when she smiled, a flash of perfect white teeth, something she began to do increasingly. She had obviously discovered that she was desirable to her husband, to whom she had been married, not long ago, when she turned fifteen, a young man in the family who ran a successful butcher's shop, whom Maya mentioned casually in the same breath with the quality of mutton at the shop. Chhaya, too, began to grow up; her churidars no longer stopped abruptly at her calves, but, elegantly, came all the way down to her ankles; and kaajal appeared around her eyes. But all this, I suspect, was her mother's and her sister's doing, and was as external to her as a frame to a painting, while Chhaya, till the last time I saw her, remained the same irresponsible and talkative girl I had known when she was nine.

The principal plaintiffs against the two sisters were the other servants. Each floor had a servants' bathroom on one side and a servants' toilet on the other; by accident the bathroom came to be on our side, while the toilet was on the side of our neighbours' flat. Our neighbour, a wealthy Sindhi widow, a simple, tall, hard lady, was specially sensitive to the insult of the toilet's proximity to her flat, a flat which, with money her son sent from Dubai, had been turned into a small palace of mirrors and marble. This situation was aggravated by Chhaya and Maya, who always went about with the privileged air of outsiders, and paid no attention to the state of that toilet. The servants complained; and, from time to time, the Sindhi lady emerged to let the two sisters know what she thought of them, and then retreated into her palace. Never have I seen people to whom a scolding mattered less than Chhaya, Maya, and their mother; only Chhaya would pretend to argue, purely for the pleasure of it, while her mother's way of showing she harboured no hurt was to, on the next day, ask for an advance on her wages.

The widow lived in the flat with her two grand-daughters. While she wore her widow's white sari with a strange pride, as if it conferred on her some special distinction, the two girls wore light, flowing dresses with elegant hems and

52

collars and button-patterns. The girls bore no resemblance to their grandmother; their faces were soft and creamy and showed signs of neither anxiety nor contentment, maturity nor innocence. They were living in that formless dream-world before marriage, where nothing was required of them but to look pretty and, in some subtle, not immediately obvious way, to prepare themselves for the future. I preferred the widow's hard masculinity. She was a bundle of insecurities, domineering and shy by turns, and, absented from her husband and son, a man and a woman in one. While her grand-daughters watched American films on video all day, and spoke the little English they did with an American accent – a sign of both ignorance and confidence – the widow spoke no English at all; and this both put her at an imagined disadvantage and gave her a conscious uprightness of bearing in that building, where everyone was a master of Bombay English. Her face gave as little relief to the eye as the landscape of Sindh from which she came. One felt she would be leading exactly this life wherever she was, whether in her village or in New York. And yet in no way did she belong to the past.

Sometimes, in the afternoon, wearing a kurta and pyjamas, I would walk down the lane and turn into the main road. The pleasure of taking a stroll in light, loose-fitting costume, without either drawing attention to myself or catching a chill, was a luxury never permitted to me in England. The sense of time on the main road, where Ambassadors passed by, and small, silent Marutis with spiteful ease, was different from that in the lane, where minutes and hours were connected to the conclusions and beginnings of phases of domestic routine. On the main road, which was only one among a family of such main roads that had joined hands to create Bombay – not the Bombay people lived in, but the one into which people emerged every day from their houses – there were cake-shops, video 'parlours', 'burger inns'. The names of these shops suggested the coming of age of a generation who were on breezy, unawed, and first-name terms with the English language. In the midst of all this, there was a bit of unexpected picturesque detail, an intrusion of rural India, in the magazine-stall, bamboo poles holding up a canopy of cloth, which sheltered a long sloping table whose entire surface was covered with magazines, the newest of which hung from a jute string that had been tied from one pole to another. The hawker was not Maharashtrian, but a North Indian in vest and dhoti, and, judging by his looks (though I do not recall his sacred thread) quite probably a brahmin. If there had been a magazine-seller sub-caste, as there was a priest sub-caste, a landowner sub-caste, and a cook sub-caste, he would have belonged to it, so completely and immemorially did he seem to be in possession of the lineaments of his trade. In the evening, he lit a hurricane lamp to illuminate the magazine covers, though there was enough light coming from the air-conditioned cake-shops to brighten the rest of the road. The magazines were filled with speculations about politicians who looked a little like the magazine seller, but lacked his sense of time and place. Together, they composed an unending Hindu epic, torn apart by incest and strife and philosophy. While the political magazines were like minutely detailed family histories, there was another kind of magazine that spoke exclusively of individuals, and described a happy secular life of evening parties and personalities that seemed as remote from government as the woodfire-lit lives of villagers. But, from time to time, the two kinds of magazine would merge into one another.

Fourteen

While reading the *Times of India* each morning, my father spares a minute for the cartoon by R. K. Laxman. While my mother is, like a magician, making untidy sheets disappear in the bedroom and producing fresh towels in the bathroom, or braving bad weather in the kitchen, my father, in the extraordinary Chinese calm of the drawing-room, is admiring the cartoon by R. K. Laxman, and, if my mother happens to be there, unselfishly sharing it with her. She, as expected, misunderstands it completely, laughing not at the joke but at the expressions on the faces of the caricatures, and at the hilarious fact that they talk to each other like human beings. On important days, Laxman occupies a large square in the centre of the newspaper, which he fills with curved or straight lines that strangely look like prime ministers and politicians, pursued by hairy, allegorical monsters called

Communalism and Corruption. On the right hand corner of the page, there is a smaller square, in which small-scale absurdities and destinies are enacted, witnessed through a window by a passer-by, hapless, moustached, bespectacled, child-like, in a dhoti and chequered jacket, he little knowing that millions regard him daily through this other wonderfully simple window around his world.

My parents knew each other from child-hood; both were born in undivided Bengal, in Sylhet, which is now in Bangladesh. In the late forties, my father went to England, and six years later, my mother; there, in London, they were married. In those days, Indian women were still a rare sight in England, and often, as the newly-married couple walked down the road, they would be stopped by an Englishman who would politely request the young man's permission to take his wife's picture. The young man would then, as he still does so often to so many things, give his good-natured and gentle assent. Prying but harmless old women would enquire, at lonely bus-stops, what the red dot on my mother's forehead signified; and for many months, a picture of her hung among other photos at a studio on Regent Street. Such a good cook was she, and such an inspired pur-chaser of herring and stewing lamb, that my poor father, neglected and underfed for six years, rap-idly gained weight and happiness after marriage. While my mother took up a full-time clerical job, my father sat for and, at last, passed his pro-fessional exams. It was while working at the India

Office, and making conversation with the large fishmonger, who called her 'love' and 'dear', and saved the pieces of turbot and halibut most precious to her, that she picked up spoken English. Like most Bengalis, she pronounces 'hurt' as 'heart', and 'ship' as 'sheep', for she belongs to a culture with a more spacious concept of time, which deliberately allows one to naively and clearly expand the vowels; and yet her speech is dotted with English proverbs, and delicate, un-Indian constructions like, 'It's a nice day, isn't it?' where most Indians would say, straightforwardly, 'It's a nice day, no?' Many of her sentences are plain translations from Bengali, and have a lovable homely melody, while a few retain their English inflections, and are sweet and foreign as the sound of whistling.

They returned to India by sea, on the Anchorline First Class. Those were the last days of the world's flatness, when, as in a map in an atlas, the continents were still embroidered upon a vast blue handkerchief of water. That fifteen-day-long, floating world between two worlds – England and India – surrounded on all sides by horizon, remains clearly in my mother's mind as a brief enchantment. What marvellous food was served, both Indian and Continental, what memorable puddings! In the evening, the ladies in saris and evening dresses, accompanied by their husbands, went out to the deck to enjoy the cool air. When darkness falls at sea, and the only light is the light on the deck on which people chat with each other as if on a promenade in a town, dressed in clothes selected after quiet and unobtrusive meditation – the selection representing some solitary, individual but habitual predeliction which only the spouse recognises – how unique, in that darkness of water and sky, must seem the human creation of evening! Every few days, there was a party at the dining-hall; a band played; others took part in musical chairs while my parents watched; often, classic films were shown. Such an air of celebration – its echo reminds me of similar occasions in my childhood, only I am not present. When I imagine my parents as they were before my birth, it is like encountering those who are both familiar and changed, like recognising, with sudden pleasure, children who have returned home after many years.

Fifteen

After Shehnaz and I had been seeing each other for about a week, I invited her to lunch at my college hall. I waited in front of the lodge, loitering invisibly while people went about, rushing, as they always do, with a special motivated speed at lunchtime. The only thing fixed in that scene was the porter, who sat inside his lodge, in a world a little detached from ours, and ignored me stolidly. When the clock struck one, I began to walk towards the hall, and Shehnaz came from behind and caught up with me, somewhat breathless. We curved round the grassy oval patch together, and entered a looming tunnel and then emerged into the second quad, with a large square of green to our right, and to our left, the L-shaped facade of the old buildings, with their consecutive staircases and rows of neighbourly windows. It must have been a warm day, for Shehnaz was wearing a white cotton top, with a message supporting the Palestinian cause printed boldly upon it, ending in a vivid exclamation mark; I noticed then how small her breasts were, two small bumps beneath her loose top, and how bony and thin she was, her collar bones radiating delicately and symmetrically beneath her neck, their outlines becoming clearer as she bent forward.

The hall had great length and depth, and yet, from the moment one joined the queue collecting trays and food, one failed to see it in perspective. That day I realised, with the disappointment one feels when discovering another person's hidden nature, that Shehnaz was a vegetarian. With a plate full of peas and salad, she stood waiting for me to pay at the till. Feeling ill at ease, we then sat facing each other at one of the interminable parallel tables that ran from one end of the hall to another. Light filled the transparent sections of the stained-glass windows. Beneath them were portraits of the dead Masters of the college, luminous presences in costume, and beneath the portraits was the table at which the Chinese graduates sat. They looked no older than boys, with straight black hair and clean, animated faces, leaning across to shout to each other in Chinese, drawing back dramatically, or lolling forward, collapsing, and settling a head upon a crooked elbow on the table. In appearance, they were more Westernised than Indians, at ease in their European clothes, industriously devouring steak and kidney pie, but they hardly spoke to the English students, forming

61

a little island at that table at lunchtime, buoyant, and full of movement. They made a domestic noise, like brothers watching a football match on television, with sounds that signified violent disagreement, or native exclamations of astonishment, but they might have been, for all I knew, discussing mathematical formulae or their syllabus. With the Chinese table as our background, Shehnaz and I ate together, more or less silently.

When we came out from the hall, we sat for some time on one of the benches on the edge of the green square, with our backs to the library windows. From there, while we talked, we could see people who had finished lunch appearing both from the hall and the Senior Common Room. Though I was not aware of it then, Mandira's room, which she had newly occupied, was behind us, over our shoulders. I would later become familiar with its rectangular window, whose shutter was lifted on hot days. On the roof above the room, there was a skylight, a narrow glass lid framed by wood, its simple, straight angles standing out against its darker background, and clearly discernible in this brief, summarised version from below. It was by this skylight that I would later identify Mandira's room.

Sixteen

The road that led to Shehnaz's college passed, at one point, over a canal. Then the road became, for a very tiny distance, a bridge, and one could sit on the wall on one side before entering the college on the left.

The canal had its own life. Ducks climbed curiously on to its bank or paddled upon the water with the utmost seriousness; twigs, branches, and leaves drifted in from the south and travelled northward. Sometimes one saw a rare polythene bag or can in the water, and, occasionally, a pair of tall, unhurried swans also headed towards a destination. Such were the daily journeys on the canal, but once, I saw two men and a woman out on a punt, laughing and shouting, and as I watched from above, the brown tops of their heads, a community of legs, and the interior of the boat with its portioned spaces and shadows became, for a few moments, visible, a glimpse of dark secrecies. On the college side, the grassy bank sloped upwards, but on the other side, there was a black wall, and the backyards of houses. When one entered the college, and began one's walk towards the rooms, one saw, to the right, across the canal, signs of domesticity seldom seen in these parts of Oxford, with its student flats and old, scholastic buildings, and elsewhere in England mainly from train windows – identical square backyards, each fencing in its peculiar organisation of clotheslines, laundry, children, cats, and women, beginning suddenly at one point and ending as suddenly at another.

Shehnaz lived on the first floor of her building, in a room even tinier and more modern than mine. Next to her bed, which during the day served as a sofa, were several shelves with books on history and politics, a few novels, picture-postcards, and photographs of her family. The books had significant titles on their spines, narrating stories of crises in faraway countries, conjuring the exciting imaginary worlds that graduates inhabit. Yet the global concerns expressed in the titles fitted in quite unremarkably with the marginal life in Shehnaz's room, with its teacups and electric kettle, and with the green, semi-pastoral life in Oxford. Opposite the bed there was a study-table, upon which stood a lamp whose angles were always crooked; beneath it, books lay open upon their backs, with lines marked out in pink and yellow, and next to that, there was a neat pencil box with pens of different colours. The table faced the wall-to-wall glass partition that illuminated every part of the small room on sunny days, and provided a seemingly unlimited view of a wide field receding slowly towards a border of trees. When one sat inside the room and looked out, one had a sense of being surrounded on all sides by space, silence, and greenery. Students in coloured jerseys sometimes played football in that field, radiating in various directions, as they did on that afternoon when Shehnaz lay on her bed and I unbuttoned her shirt. On such brilliant days, unusual birds could be seen running on the field, especially when it was empty and hot and shadowless, and full of its own presence. Along its sides, beautiful English flowers bloomed in clusters, and if one walked there, one encountered small, timid creatures, shy hedgehogs and nervous, preoccupied squirrels. Whenever I looked up that afternoon, I would become aware of the frame of the window, which created an illusory and transparent separation between ourselves and the day outside. It was impossible not to be conscious of nature and sky, not to be surprised at how incidental, like stage-sets, these rooms were, and how specific the human rehearsals within them, of love or social intercourse. Our privacy, carefully constructed in the room, lost its meaning against the background of the glass that continually let in the solitude of that landscape.

Seventeen

The walls in Mandira's room had photographs stuck to them with Blu-tack, and posters of Great Britain, showing the interiors of churches and cathedrals, and pieces of paper that had verses typed upon them. Greeting cards from friends all over the world were arranged upon the mantelpiece, and on the wall opposite, by the window, there was a board to which was pinned an amazing array of scribbled messages, lecture-lists, and printed or handwritten invitations from acquaintances, tutors, college societies, and the students' union. There seemed to be a great crowd of people scattered through the colleges of Oxford with whom Mandira was on first-name terms; later, when her life became more solitary, more nocturnal, and was spent more upon the anxieties we created for ourselves, those letters still stayed pinned to the board, no longer representing her other life outside her room, but a forgetfulness, the dates missed, the events long over, but the lecture-lists and invitation cards remaining upon the board as a beguiling and innocent surface.

In Oxford, the modes of social existence are few but tangible. But the tangibleness of this existence – conversing at parties, studying at libraries, going to lectures – is at the same time dreamlike. Sometimes the occasions seem like images that one has projected from within for one's own entertainment, until they fade, as they must after a certain hour at night. Night brings darkness, the emptying of the images that made up the day, so that, in the solitary moment before falling asleep, the day, and Oxford, seem to be a dream one is about to remember. At this moment, one knows that one has no existence for others in Oxford, just as others have no existence for oneself, except in their absence. Daylight and waking bring the feeling of having travelled great distances, of arriving, at last, at a place that is not home, a feeling that cannot be exactly recalled or understood later, but which occurs at the same time each morning, until one gets out of bed, changes into one's trousers and shirt, and leaves the room. To be someone's lover, to share someone's bed, does not help, but only disturbs that fragile configuration of events and meetings, that neutral and desirable intersection of public places and private ambition, that creates the surface of the dream; instead, the moments of solitariness and self-consciousness, such as before sleeping and at waking, begin to recur unexpectedly, interrupting the flow and allocation of time, of schedules, deadlines, and appointments. One begins to get distanced from Oxford; more and more, one sees it as one's own dream, an illusion or vision composed relentlessly of others, but not shared by anyone else. This is in part an effect of knowing that one's relationship with one's lover could have only taken place in Oxford, and has no meaning outside it, and that Oxford itself is a temporal and enchanted territory that has no permanence in one's life.

Mandira lived in a college among undergraduates. The rhythms and inflections, the sounds, were different here from those of graduate life. For one thing, the internationalism of a graduate building was missing; most of the undergraduates were English, and, speaking in accents that belonged to different but neighbouring localities and regions, they formed a kind of family, constantly on the move, opening and closing doors, engaging in interminable exchanges in the corridor, and borrowing each other's provisions. There was an urgency and panic in much of what they did, writing weekly essays and preparing for examinations, and tension exploded either into laughter, or remained unexpressed as silent resentment. Men and women mixed with each other in large, friendly groups, but there was also a subdued tension between the sexes that came out in their jokes, an undercurrent of signals and hidden priorities that never existed in quite such a way in graduate life. Later, I came to know that many of

Mandira's English girlfriends, whom I would sometimes find in her room drinking tea, speaking a rapid language that I hardly followed, were always falling in and out of love with the men on their floor or their staircase, and a conversation with a female friend was only a stop-gap between two sexual moments of anxiety or pleasure. Heartbreak was usual; for about a month, one would see a certain combination of singles and couples on the staircase, the single people in jeans and the couples often dressed in black formal clothes for guest-night; and then the combination would change; the male would disappear, and the woman would return to her plain skirt and woollen jumper. For graduates, there is no real difference between term-time and the breaks in between; and, as most of them come from other continents, home is too far away to go back to; so they stay on in Oxford during the shorter vacations, going to libraries, continuing their research. But the undergraduates keep returning home to the coasts of England, or to the North, or to Wales, in the winter and Easter breaks, home, where, one gathers from their talk, happiness or unhappiness is a more unsurprising, everyday affair than here, home, where one speaks another language, with sister and mother and father; a simple train-journey takes them there, and brings them back, changed somewhat, redder or a little less thin, or with their hair cut much shorter. When they are away, the colleges become monuments, stone passages and stairways, empty halls and gardens, a place that is something between a deserted monastery and an unused bed-and-breakfast guest-house, a world made of Latin inscriptions and dates upon walls, and neatly made beds in rooms with no one in them.

But strange things happen even in term-time. Once, I remember, someone died, a former boyfriend of one of Mandira's friends, a young man of twenty-one, a 'commoner' of the college; he had died alone in his room, strangely, of a heart-attack. At lunchtime, I had seen some students crying, and then, that evening, when Mandira told me the story, the correspondences began to fit. That episode, unknown to most graduates, hung over the college and Mandira's staircase for about a week. It was about at that time that things began between Mandira and myself, without either of us knowing where they would lead to. She would lock her door and come and sit beside me on the bed. If one of her friends happened to knock, and call out, 'Mandira!', we would both be silent; we would listen to the scratching on the notepaper outside, and smile as the person walked away. She wanted very much to make love to me, and at night, after switching off the light, she would lie, small and warm, underneath her blankets. She was completely new to love, unexpectedly bold in her various pleas and demands, and ashamed at the wrong moments. Our blinded gropings were more exploratory than passionate, for both of us were inexperienced, and a little afraid of what was supposed to happen at the end of this act. These were the only moments when we were tolerant of each other's disabilities and short-comings. Just above the bed there was a skylight that let a glow into the room, so that we could see each other's outlines, and the reassuring shapes of certain objects.

Eighteen

At the end of Cornmarket Street, near the Lloyd's Bank, comes a confluence of four roads, making an irregular sort of cross which one could possibly see from an aircraft. There is no centre in Oxford, only different points of reference, from each of which the conception of the city is altered slightly. Thus one never feels completely rooted, and ascending three floors in a building of the New Bodleian Library gives one, before entering the reading-room, a view of Holywell Street from above. One senses, from that window, how distinct and well marked-out each section of the city is, each partially unknown to the other, each potentially undiscovered to its own inhabitants – for, from above, Holywell Street, with its repetitive up-and-down movement of cyclists and pedestrians, the faint white fringe of its pavement, and the houses on either side appearing quite oddly rearranged from this angle, seems, in the disturbing perspective gained by height and distance, continually strange, a place that will never become familiar or old. The orderly, disappearing line of traffic, the activity on the roads, harmonious and self-dispersing, the unreality of the scene and one's relationship with its unreality, are exposed and encompassed by this view from a third-storey window, which reveals absences between one lane and another, one house and another, untenanted, unexplainable spaces, and that absence over all these, on eye-level with the window, so that the places one has walked through or passed daily lose their known features. It takes something as small and unsuspected as this, a change of view and altitude, to bring one's foreignness to one's self, the feeling of being separated from the routines that one thought attached one to the city, of being secretly in transit. Similarly, at the junction of four roads at the end of Cornmarket Street, the minor change in gradient of one of the roads, St Aldate's, the way it dips downward, so that the line at its end is known to be a false line, a border concealing and sheltering a second and more distant border at that end of the city, marks, in the midst of everything, an unnoticed but real departure. In a city so little known, so full of such instants, such escapes, events and the memory of events become temporary stays; Shehnaz, Mandira's room, the walks taken together, a meeting with Sharma, reassure one that one has not been in Oxford alone, that one has shared it with others, till the solitary

73

experience of being in transit returns, and friends and acquaintances are borne away by this city, which renews itself, and becomes, once more, strange to oneself. It is the city that remains, a kind of meeting place, modern and without identity, but deceptively archaic, that unobtrusively but restlessly realigns its roundabouts and lanes and landmarks, so that it never becomes one's own, or anyone else's.

The long road adjacent to St Aldate's is the High Street. One of my earliest meetings with Shehnaz was when we ran into each other at the junction, and she was going the opposite way, into High Street, in search of a florist; I hardly knew her then, but on her request, turned back to walk with her. The florist's was closed, so it must have been evening, one of the long, bright evenings of summer. On both sides of this road are ancient colleges, with grey steps and wooden doors and grim, outdated windows, smooth brown stone walls, clock towers and spires. The gong of the clocks, especially the one at the Cornmarket Street end of High Street, can be heard every hour with great and transparent clarity, and at night, when I would hear the ever-increasing repetition from Mandira's room, I would become conscious of the strangeness of the place I was about to fall asleep in, of distance, and the suspension of activity. As one walks past the colleges on High Street, one glimpses, through the frame of the doorway, another frame, which marks off the end of the entrance area with the porter's lodge, noticeboards, and mail-room, broadening out into the first quad with its empty oval or square of green, its generously enclosed, yet strangely liberated, parameter of open air and space, the façade of a building, with the college chapel, behind the green, and a measured rectangle of sky. This is the abbreviated, painting-like view that passers-by have of the interiors of the colleges, and the rest is hidden behind an edifice of stone that is part history and part fantasy, and has little to do with the domestic or working lives of students, and their particular slang or vernacular. Yet the students do not really matter, because within the college walls there is a world – a geography and a weather – that clings to its own time and definition and is changed by no one. In this world, glimpsed briefly by the passer-by through the open doorway, a certain light and space and greyness of stone, and at night, a certain balance of lamplight, stone, and darkness, co-exist almost eternally, and it is the students, with their nationalities and individual features, their different voices and accents, their different habits and attempts at adjustment, their sense of bathos and possession of reality, who, in truth, vanish, are strangely negated, so that, when the passer-by later remembers what he saw, the students seem blurred, colourful, accidental, even touching, but constantly skirting the edge of his vision, while it is possible to clearly and unequivocally recall the dignity and silence of the doorway and the world beyond it.

A little further on, a short distance before Magdalen Bridge, are the Queen's Lane Coffee Shop and a newsagent's on the left, and the Examination Schools to one's right. On certain days in May and June, examinees in black gowns, at half-past twelve and five-thirty, trickle out, and then overflow, on to High Street from the entrance of the Schools, the women in black skirts and white shirts, some jubilantly holding bouquets in their hands, the men in white shirts and black trousers, faces and outlines merging on the pavement and then separating at street-corners, a young man materialising from the crowd and awkwardly crossing the street in the midst of the traffic, sweethearts, their faces flushed with pride and anxiety, waving madly and then embracing, large groups chattering and breaking up, and other smaller groups held close in serious conference. This is one of the few occasions on which one sees something common to all these faces; before one's eyes, for the first time, a network of friendships is formed, correspondences that link acquaintances and strangers in one milling and crowded moment, that is already turning into the past, already disintegrating only to be remembered as something so immediate as not to be wholly real; for no one, later, actually knows what it was like at that moment. Common to each, as they emerge, is the nervous or successful air of opera-singers; for each one has been privileged and chosen by Oxford to perform for it; and now that unique and invigorating moment, for better or for worse, is

76

over. On the other side, life at the newsagent's goes on as before; polite people, such as those one holds the door open for, say 'Thank you' and leave with newspapers and sandwiches. By chance, one might pass them on the street a month later, an encounter that does not bring up a memory or a connection, but something in their place, neither a memory or a connection, which causes one's identity to reconstitute itself. The newsagent's sells postcards of Oxford, small, shining squares with pictures of colleges, hidden lanes, the Radcliffe Camera, and students on bicycles. The postcards are weightless, but palpable, and when one stops to look at them, they have a recognisability that one's consciousness of Oxford lacks; they seem more real than the place one has lived in.

Nineteen

When my parents moved to that lane in the Christian area in the suburbs of Bombay, I was in Oxford; I did not witness the moving. In the summer, I returned for my vacations to a house I had not seen before, but only read about in letters, a tidy flat on the third floor that was smaller than the flats I had lived in all my life when my father worked in his company.

Once, when I was sleeping late into the morning in my new room, I was woken by an insistent metallic noise, something between a hammering and a ringing. The door at the end of the room opened on to a veranda, and when I went out, I saw a rubbish truck standing in the lane, an old, obsolete truck, such as one always sees on the roads in India, with no roof except in the front, where the driver's seat is. Men who appeared to be dressed only in undergarments – vests and shorts – were clambering busily over the rubbish that had already been piled in the open section of the truck, and were now leaning in a carefree way with their elbows on one side of the truck, and looking out at the lane. The tallest man among them was standing just outside the gate to our building, and with cheeky disregard continually beating a plate with what might have been a spoon. He stood rooted to the spot, and, because he was wearing shorts, I could see how thin his legs were, with hairless knees, bent at a concave angle because of the firmness with which he was standing. The rude noise he was making sent the sweeper-women of the building, pretty girls among them, into a panic; with worried faces, clutching large plastic bins, they were hurrying towards the truck, from which the little men in undergarments were leaning out and looking at them insolently. There was something sexual in the air, and this ritual repeated itself at this time on almost every day of the week.

I grew to love that lane. The flat was on the third floor, and its veranda brought one marginally closer to its life. There was commerce between our building and the shops on the main road, from which barefoot errand boys would come carrying newspapers, provisions, video cassettes, and bottles of soda, taciturn, dark adolescents who wore t-shirts handed down by their employers, with 'USA', 'Smile', or 'Beat King' printed upon them. In this part of the city, with its small-town atmosphere, taxis were rivalled by auto-rickshaws, manic, hooded three-wheelers that were good for short distances. At the local station, these autos arrived incessantly in a cloud of dust before a queue of passengers, who, one by one, were carried off through a series of jolts and shocks towards the various roads radiating around Bandra – Linking Road, Turner Road, Hill Road, Khar. And one would come in the afternoon, every few days, to the gate outside our building, and either Mohan or my guru, or both, would alight from its tiny, semi-visible, confessional-like interior, and pay the impatient auto driver. From the veranda, their entrance into the compound was visible at close-quarters, and the sudden roar with which the auto disappeared always left me unprepared.

My parents lived here for three years. During my first summer visit, walking down the parallel lanes, I found by-lanes connecting one lane to another. On either side of these by-lanes, which were like shrunken versions of the bigger ones, miniature portraits of them, there were old cottages, and, around them, a distinct island of life that had formed by itself, consisting of cats, shrubs, birds, and an absence of people. I was always grateful for, without knowing precisely why, the detour of passing through these by-lanes.

It was Chitrakaki, my mother's friend, who, having lived in the suburbs for thirty years, introduced my parents to a new family doctor in the area, someone who would make house-calls. He was a short Marathi gentleman called Dr Deshpande, long threads of black hair combed across his disproportionately visible scalp, square-jawed, stout, bespectacled, with, disconcertingly, dimples appearing on his cheeks when he smiled. Like all general practitioners who are slaves to their patients and available at their beck and call at all hours of the day, he had no degree but his MBBS; he was more a Samaritan than a doctor; his arrival was met with relief rather than apprehension. He was not consulted for serious illnesses, but for headaches, stomach-upsets, and indigestion, and for his company he charged fifty rupees less than the doctors in the city. This part of the suburbs was his natural terrain; he was linked by phone to a wide variety of sufferers, and was in demand everywhere. He usually made only one diagnosis, 'There's a virus in the air this time of the year,' but if one disagreed with him, he had no objection to changing it.

Chitrakaki lived not far away in a rented flat on the ground floor of a two-storeyed house with her husband, son, daughter-in-law, two dogs, and a cat. Once she owned a rooster which, strange plant, was convinced it was human and insisted upon being introduced to her friends. The dogs – a fox terrier that died, a dachshund that met its end in a road-accident, two hairy pekinese – Chitrakaki and her husband loved and cared for like their own children. And they forever remained children, even when they had become old, scuffling underneath the dining-table and barking their hearts out at the wall-lizard. In other ways they were shockingly dog-like; for the mother pekinese and her son, Chitrakaki once related lovingly, had become husband and wife, and then had had puppies. Each time, during those thirty years, when a bitch had puppies, Chitrakaki witnessed their blind, recumbent birth, and then gave them away.

She loved my mother's cooking. Whistling (she had learnt how to whistle in England, where both she and her husband had met my father as a penniless student), she would loiter carelessly in the kitchen, looking askance as my mother gave the cook instructions, vainly, and stealthily, trying to sniff out the recipe. When she tried it at home, however, it was never, never right. She was convinced my mother had cruelly held back something, a seemingly unimportant but crucial ingredient she had quite premeditatedly forgotten to tell her. My mother made things from peelings, fish-heads, dried fish. It was East Bengali cuisine, with its origins in villages on drought and flood-hit riversides, a poor man's diet, perfected by people who could not afford to throw away even the skin of a white-gourd or the head of a fish, transformed into food by adding oil and garlic and chilli paste and poppy seed and common salt.

The people who really belonged to our lane were those who were on its margins – servants, sweepers, watchmen, hawkers of vegetable and fish who sent their cries out to the balconies and went with their baskets from door to door, even the beggars who, like the tradesmen, worked on a repeated route within a definite area. There was a Christian woman who, wearing the same tattered white dress, stood outside the building gates every week and sang a tuneless song in disjointed English. English was spoken quite naturally here by the poor, many of whom were Christians, and said their prayers in the language.

Gradually, the area changed. New buildings, like ours, came up where the oldest cottages used to be, concrete structures with sequences of black holes that would become flats in which people and children would live, the rooms, kitchens, and bathrooms still unrecognisable, each building looking at this stage like a huge birdhouse. The labourers sat and chipped away at the large rocks with their chisels, while their womenfolk, with saris tucked around their knees, bent down and scooped tiny black stones into a metal plate; some of them sat apart, nursing babies, the breast hidden by the child's head, one end of the sari pulled forward, held aloft, and used as a kind of curtain to an imaginary room. The stray dogs of the lane were friendly with the children, who would pummel them fearlessly with tiny fists, or race them down the lane, while the dogs took such pestering wisely and accommodatingly. This floating community, infants and all, disappeared every year, and then they, or another very like them, reappeared on another site. Often, they would live in improvised shelters they had built themselves. From the rear-balcony of our flat, one could see a building coming up in an adjoining space, where our compound had ended with a wall. On this side of our house, clothes were left to dry on the balcony, and there were garages downstairs in which tenants' cars were kept. The atmosphere here was in contrast to that of the front side, where cars and people kept coming in.

At different points of time in those three years, a maidservant and a cook who worked in our flat began to visit the rear-balcony in the afternoons with an aimless look in their eyes. Both had made a long-distance, incommunicado relationship of looks and gestures with someone on the building site. There was some doubt about this at first, but on one definitive occasion, my parents were told by an informer – perhaps the sweeper-woman – that the cook (who, before she found love, was a slow-moving, turtle-like woman with luxuriant hips) had made a friendship with a Nepali watchman, a matter of waves, smiles, and glimpses, but then a serious affair of meetings when she would disappear from the house for what she thought were unnoticeable intervals. Returning, she would say she had been to the toilet. Romance was dead among the middle classes, but among domestic servants it was still a disruptive force, giving them a secret life that had the fraught emotions, the atmosphere and the singing beauty of old Hindi films. When a servant fell in love, the implications were felt all over the house, and became a subject of conversation; my guru would interrupt his tuition to speak about these matters of the heart, glancing sideways when the servant being discussed entered the room.

Meanwhile, the new houses were completed.

Each family, in those matchbox-like flats, put up paintings, placed decorations on the window-sills, hung up lamp-shades, as if life, taken out of the bundle of cloth in which it had been hurriedly wrapped, had settled down and resumed its ordinariness. As the cottages fell, and buildings came up, Hindus moved into the area to live alongside the Christians – Sindhis, a tall, migratory business people, who brought with them a passion for cars and noisy weddings, extended families consisting of grandsons and cousins, and women-folk who sang an unimpassioned, strangely tranquil, version of devotionals in the evening; hovering wistfully somewhere on the border of tunefulness, it brought the quality of a faraway time and place to the area. By the time my parents decided they could no longer live in Bombay, and in those months of waiting for the flat to be sold, until at last when they packed up everything, leaving every room with crates full of possessions, the character of the lane changed perceptibly.

Twenty

That year, full of those odd coincidences that brought Shehnaz and Mandira and me together, my parents moved from Bombay to Calcutta.

Calcutta is my birthplace. It is the only city I know that is timeless, where change is naturalised by the old flowing patterns, and the anxiety caused by the passing of time is replaced by fatigue and surrender. It is where my father, having left Sylhet, came as a student fifty years ago. Those were the last years before independence; and my father lived in a hostel in North Calcutta. He ate great quantities of rice in the canteen, and never left a fish-head uneaten. He was an only child, parentless, in this city where people spoke Bengali differently and more coldly than he did. North Calcutta was then classical and beautiful, with Central Avenue and the colleges of Tropical Medicine and other sciences, the imposing colonial buildings, the institutions of learning and the roads matching the nobility of their names. And my father saw that nobility with his own eyes. In all the world then he had nobody. It was before history was born, and he himself became who he was, studying in a city that is always pre-natal, pre-nascent. The tiny village in East Bengal he was born in, with its village school he went to in early childhood, seems to have never existed. It is now on the other side of the border, in Bangladesh. It is as if my father came into being from fantasy, like an image, in 1923. Yet it is an image full of truth, to think of him studying in Calcutta, or taking a tram-ride, one of the marginal, anonymous people who were neighbours with history, one of the millions, studying, discussing politics, listening to songs, living in hostel rooms, eating in the 'cabins' of North Calcutta, who were bypassed and yet changed, without their names or the quality of those moments ever being known, by independence and partition. So India took on a new shape, and another story began, with homelands becoming fantasies, never to be returned to or remembered. What did it mean to him, then, without brother and sister, alone, to be part of so many? He loved that life. When Tagore died, millions flowed through the streets, some taking turns to be pall-bearers, some surging forward to touch his feet or his body and then being left behind while others took their place, my father one of those who had momentary proximity to the dead poet, touching him before he disappeared from view, so that, whenever Ray's documentary on Tagore is shown on television, my mother leans forward towards the end of the film and peers at the screen to catch a glimpse of my father. Thousands, without name or face, but known perhaps to one other person somewhere else, appeared and disappeared around the body of the dead poet held aloft, indistinguishable from each other, weaving in and out of that moment.

Strange to think that a poet should have suddenly brought to the world's brief attention a small corner of the earth, where a rounded, musical tongue was spoken, where freshwater fish was eaten daily and its bones sorted nimbly with the fingers, where small, earnest men walked in white dhotis with tender, overlapping folds in the heat. An unknown tongue, unknown emotions, strange, impoverished Bengal! From the dense forests and swamps of the Sundarbans, to the magical place, Kalighat, a port and a people grew, a poet and singer in each family, ideals and romance and the love of art nurtured among these frail quick-tempered people, and the wide Hooghly flowing in the midst of all this. Wide rivers, the Hooghly and the Padma, with indistinct horizons on either side, a constant thoroughfare for river-transport and civilization, with lonely passages of water and horizon where ferrymen journeyed from one side to the other.

For many years, my father's family was hardly known to me. Two portraits, of my grandfather and grandmother, hung upon the wall above the doorway to my parents' bedroom in the houses we lived in. The family had once been landowners, and then they scattered and gradually became poor, settling down in towns on this side of the border, while the great house became a memory in Bangladesh, with a few relatives still living in it. I remember in childhood travelling with my parents to a town in Assam, and being taken in a car to the outskirts, and entering a place without electricity, where people lived in a small house among other houses; we were greeted by a family: a father, his daughter, her husband, and a child, and the old man had the same surname as I. My father addressed him with the Bengali word for 'paternal uncle', and they spoke in the Sylheti dialect, and fragments of that world in which the remnants of my father's family lived came alive in the light of a hurricane-lamp.

My father's ancestral village was on the banks of a tributary of the Surma. To leave that village and approach the outside world one must use the waterway and the canoe, and emerge eventually into another world. Heat, mud, water, the flight of water-insects, roots holding the earth, women washing clothes, their heads covered by saris, ponds made green by water-hyacinth, the flat, wide sails of the lotus – such images come to me of journeying down that river. It is a Bengal that missed the changes taking place elsewhere, the middle-class reforms of Brahmoism, the intellectual movements in Hinduism. More important,

there, than the secular nationalist figures, Rammo-
hun Roy and Tagore, initiators of modern Bengali
culture, was a native strain of Vaishnavism, the
worship of Krishna, Ganesh, Parvati, an ecstatic
love of their images, sung out in unwritten songs
and poems.

To that strain of worship my father's family
belongs. Dispersed though they were over Eastern
and Northern India, from Cachhar to Brindaban,
rarely in contact with each other, second cousins
and third cousins and uncles, some dead,
uprooted from tradition, a refugee people, I would
hear of singers and painters in every branch of the
family, and once, on a visit to a remote part of
India when I was a child, I received blessings and
a book of poems from my father's aunt; it was a
book she had written herself. That family, perhaps
because once so rich, was little in touch with
education; my father's aunt had never been to
school; her Bengali was self-taught. Their love of
poetry was not created by the new secular rever-
ence for culture and literature that came with
Tagore, but was an indigenous offshoot of a long
line of ecstatic worship and craftsmanship. Not
very long ago, in the summer, after my parents
had moved to Calcutta, we made a trip to where
my father's aunt's son now lived, with his sister
and her daughter, in a barely recognisable lane off
a small road beyond the highway at Dum Dum.
They were overjoyed to see us; on the veranda
to the small house, canvases rested, portraits
of saints and holy men and women. My

cousin was an artist, and all his paintings were devotional. On the veranda there was a table on which there were lumps of clay that looked like turds but became, on closer inspection, little animals, bulls, cows, and images of Krishna. These my cousin took me by my hand to show me proudly. Knowing my love of music, he had taken out harmonium and tablas, and urged me and my mother to sing. Then they themselves sang with little prompting, from a vast repertoire of songs in both Hindi and Bengali, some of which they had composed themselves. An anxious, child-like joy in their own creations lived in that house. In a room at the back, my cousin was working upon a commissioned sculpture of a living saint; made from clay, to life-like measurements, sitting cross-legged upon newspapers spread out on a table, it was an ecstatic moulding for worship. Creation was worship; that family was excited and full of love for that image; they had made it together, my cousin doing the sculptor's work while his sister and her child helped him to hold it still and achieve its proportions. It was still unpainted, its colour the colour of clay, but the eyes of the saint and the expression of his face and body no longer belonged to earth and mud but to the realm of the imagination. For the first time I could see where my own private joys came from – the love of songs, of music, of pride and delight in creation. That delight is my family's gift.

Twenty One

Cowley Road, Iffley Road, and St Clement's – small, mean, jaunty families live here side by side with the Bangladeshis and Pakistanis. This is the tribe that belonged to Dickensian alleys, the aboriginal community that led its island-life, its daily routines and struggles, and scarcely heard of Empire or took part in governance. For them the supermarkets were built, to work in and to shop at. Not Sainsbury's, but Tesco, with its long aisles of shopping trolleys, sides of beef and ham, frozen chips, mango chutney, and spinach at tuppence less. Towards such centres they gravitate, living in a perpetual present, and then walk home to their houses with tiny gardens. Not for them history, old buildings, literature, but an England of small comforts and marriages, happy or unhappy. For them, television, with endless runs of Eastenders and Coronation Street, showing them their lives and those of their children. There is a church here, in Cowley, for they are devout Christians, drinking Protestants, religious not in a theological but in a family way, with roles allocated to the sexes, the men believing, and supporting their football team, the women praying, and going out shopping, all of them seeming to know the words of the Sunday hymns by heart, but blaspheming and cursing God when they feel like it. Speaking an English that is hardly spoken in any other part of the world any more, with queer proverbs and turns, dropped consonants and vowels, turning the language like meat inside their mouths.

For them the cans of beer with German names, and black Guinness. Turners of nuts and bolts, sweepers of a clean country, the young men white and unnaturally fat on baked potatoes and cheddar cheese, still pathetically dependent on their mothers, the women wearing dresses, their feet either in high-heels or sandals in the cold, their legs unstockinged in winter, secretly shaved, with faint blue and purple veins, the older men with long, combed, wavy hair, wearing coats and flared trousers, seldom unshaven, never tying their hair in a pony-tail like the students, rarely seen in corduroys, the last chain-smokers and meat-eaters of England, thin, smartly dressed, energetic, hanging around street-corners, escaped from their wives and children, looking like snooker-players, white men leading black lives. White niggers, they fought the war, sang drinking songs, married, died. Not for them cars, but the

93

great public transport system, joining and holding communities and families together, the buses coming every twenty minutes. They are the ones who lived in a world of horrible and immediate prejudices, coined the terms 'Paki' and 'wog', and then lived side by side with the Patels and Muslim Bangladeshi families, and worked for their sons who look like Latin Americans and chatter in Cockney amongst themselves. For them a diet of Brain's faggots and frozen peas, the middle-aged skinheads, in the nineties, become fathers with children perched on their shoulders, the punks, with their phosphorescent hair, vanished like a seasonal insect. For them, recreation is the desolately green area of the Headington Parks, pleasure a public piss in a public toilet, and misery an hour spent in the launderette. This world is a different world from that of the University; they never meet. The state of intoxication here, broken bottles, a beggar's foul breath, is more basic than the students' social drunkenness, a state of the soul.

Whenever I have come here, it has rained. Clouds gather at this end, little England. The City centre is charming, like a picture, and the lanes off Broad Street, off Jesus and Lincoln colleges, are romantic and small, eighteenth century exteriors with twentieth century fittings, romantic lamplight and mist. But here even the pubs are different. Once, finding myself at this end of town, out on an edge, I entered one; it was a weekday. It was quiet and uncrowded; people seemed to have gathered here as a matter of course, as if it were a

94

second home; they noticed me, but said nothing. Bright wallpaper on the walls; tables and chairs; coffee was served; an old man sat in a chair by a window and the entrance, ignoring a draught, ignoring newcomers, a large Alsatian dog by his side, his only companion. It must have been nine o'clock, and yet the pub was relaxed and half-empty. It had no designer photographs of old cricketers, no designer posters of old advertisements for the London Tube, for Coca Cola, for the Festival Hall; its atmosphere belonged to itself; it was like an old house. The young men and women, couples talking with each other, looked different from the students; their hair was straight and limp; they had never been to the orthodontist as children; raised teeth, and lines around their mouths, gave their faces an odd softness. Their complexion, too, was white; they seemed like Madame Tussaud's waxworks, a lost world, remade and fixed. And yet this was their world.

Sometimes, in the evening, I would be confronted by alcoholics who, for some reason, seemed least ill-at-ease when begging from a dark-skinned foreigner. If I parted with a coin, I would receive a 'Thank you, sir' in return, and if I refused, I would either be wished good luck or cursed for being in England. Once I was cursed for being a student by a beggar I had become friendly with: 'There's no difference between you and me, mate, we're both dossing around on other people's money.' And I remember an elderly gentleman whom I saw both in Cowley and in North Oxford, drunk every time, a myopic who wore spectacles with a strong, dark frame that gave his face a learned look which in itself is an anachronism in a University town where most students wear contact lenses.

On dry days, furniture would be piled outside the second-hand shops on Cowley Road. The pavement would be filled with wardrobes, armchairs, sofas, dressing-tables with mirrors, lampstands, in a space next to a bus-stop, where a strange woman would come to a man and say, 'Could you spare me your cigarette-end?' Certain areas were marked out and separated from the rest by smells of Kentucky Fried Chicken. Then, at last, came the Cowley Market Hall, part hardware and stationery store, and part a derelict precursor to the supermarket, a solid, unpolished shell where couples wandered to buy things – children's toys, a hammer, writing-paper, liquorice. And, as one walked on and came marginally closer to London, this would end, these lives, with their idiosyncracies, laughter, pressures, and sorrows, portrayed forty years ago in the black and white Ealing comedies and dramas, no grand characters in those films, only unforgettable bit-parts, bit-characters, all this would empty out into the road turning right towards the John Radcliffe Hospital, or going straight past an elevation, green and wide and sloping upward, a public common where East Oxford seemed to vanish. *It Always Rains On Sunday*, both the title and the film itself express what goes on inside these houses, women with

96

husbands they both love and do not love, memories of old beaus, old sweethearts, sudden extremities, sudden panic, then routine reasserting itself, and the rain that always hangs over these streets. Then, as the film ends, so does this small world, in a great vent and opening of space.

Twenty Two

When I told Mandira that 'Private Shop' on Cowley Road was a sex-shop, she was curious to see it; she had never been in one before. I never took her there, though; it remained one of our many promised destinations. Anyway, it was difficult to get in without being noticed; and when one opened the door, a bell tinkled as in a drugstore in old American films. A man, pale, cheaply well-dressed, one of life's jetsam, stood behind the counter, appearing to fidget busily with something, nodding and saying 'Can I help?' as you entered, as if you were just another customer and this just another shop, and then, as you looked around and became briefly engrossed, he would avoid, out of consideration, looking at your eyes, trying not to appear contemptuous, but anxious to confide and be truthful when asked questions. Magazines, three for the price of one, phone numbers, giggly dildos, pink perpendicular rubber organs arranged like confectionary, brought feelings, inside one, of surprise, laughter, and embarrassment. It was because it excited the first two emotions especially that it might have been a place for a couple to amuse themselves, but when I went there, I went alone; its wonders remained undiscovered by Mandira.

There were many promises to her I did not keep, promises to go to new places, towns, sleepy English villages, to vanish from Oxford for a holiday. And then there was her wish to discover, through me, herself, for her a heartfelt but simple demand, for me, almost impossible to comply. She would have had me possess her, to commit to extinction both our selves, while I always held back, selfishly, on the brink, refusing to take refuge inside her. So it was that we lived for a time in that space in which bodies exist on the borders of each other, separated by flesh, by the life of each, which, unadmitted by both, is actually moving in its own direction, towards its own future. In this way, we teetered on the brink of each other, and her desire remained superfluous and unfulfilled.

After a spell of depression, she decided to postpone her finals by a year; in Trinity term, she moved out of the college, packed her things in two suitcases and left while her friends prepared for their exams. She moved to a house in a blind lane off Cowley Road, a room with a wide, springy double-bed, light pink walls, and tiny curtained squares that were windows. The house had a path, not more than ten feet long, leading to its door, and before the path there was a small unsteady wooden gate, of a child's height, purely ornamental in nature, which would have kept nobody out. The house was owned by an old English widow with white hair and grey eyes, a sort of harmless English witch who looked as if she practised on the ouija board, but actually only nagged Mandira to remember to close the front door, to buy her own washing liquid, to pay her rent on time, to receive no calls after ten-thirty, and who had dinner at six and watched television thereafter. She let out her rooms upstairs to students, or to anyone for that matter, for Mandira's neighbour was a woman who worked all night and slept during the day.

Mandira then began to live more or less alone, cut off from her old friends, her college routines, and her tutor, an old don in spectacles. The only person who visited her then, besides me, who would drop by dutifully from time to time, was a nineteen-year-old English boy from college, awkward, inarticulate, his eyes hidden by a mop of hair, who loved Mozart and Beethoven, who communicated with Mandira by simply 'being around', by smiles, by listening as she talked of her problems, by nodding in agreement and uttering monosyllables to support his nods, by running her small errands, by making silent gestures like lending her his pullover. His name was Simon. He became even more silent and reserved when I was there, and remained, throughout, a witness to the precarious way in which our involvement began, and then the way it dwindled. He was one of the few English students in Oxford with working-class origins; his old parents, whose only son he was, lived in Dover; his father was a trombone-player in a four-man band. Simon was doing physics, one of those things you cannot learn, but must have an aptitude for. Of all Mandira's friends, he remained the most faithful to her, accepted her as she was, overlooked her shortcomings; towards the end, he even transmitted to her his love of classical music, and I would find her sometimes, listening, with a self-conscious expression, to a Beethoven sonata.

Then, to supplement her scholarship money, Mandira began to work in the Covered Market, part-time jobs at a florist's, and a cake-shop, for which she did not require a work-permit. In the morning, she would cycle to her library. After lunch, she would walk to Turl Street, and then enter the market, and, once inside her shop, she would wear a white apron over her clothes, and a white cap on her head, the uniform at the cake-shop. Because she was so fair, she looked almost, though not quite, English behind the counter; whenever I visited her, I bought a pastry or a tart, and she could not resist smiling at the nature of our meeting, the ridiculousness of her apparition in such a uniform, for she seemed, at such moments, to see herself from the outside. The lady at the shop, as the widow whose house she lived in, would ask her occasionally, 'Is he your boyfriend?' to which she would say, half pleased and half exasperatedly, 'No, not really.'

Through her I became familiar with the Covered Market, with the intricacy and timelessness of its organisation, its hours of business, when it served as a thoroughfare for students passing between Broad Street and High Street, its fixed closing-time of five o'clock, when the iron gates on both sides were shut and locked. Who would have thought, surrounded on almost every side by colleges, Jesus, Lincoln, and Oriel not too far away, Broad Street, Blackwell's, and the Sheldonian on the other side, that here there was a place of buying and selling, a place that both quickened and constricted the appetite? For, not far away from the sweet-smelling, moist floors of the florist's were the butchers' shops with sticky larders and clotted blood, dead pheasants swinging upside down from hooks, fragrant carcasses, pig's livers and trotters. Here, then, exposed, was the dark Anglo-Saxon love of offal which went back centuries. In another part of the market were stalls with stacked yards of silk, folded around a flat board, and the old system of measure here, and the way the shopkeepers busily touched and tested the cloth with their fingers, reminded me of the stalls of New Market in Calcutta, where people still speak of cloth in terms of the human body, and still speak sometimes of one or two 'hands' of cloth. Mandira worked, from two to four o'clock, in the midst of all this activity. For that period of time, she became, unquestioningly, part of that small community of shopkeepers, attendants, helpers, girls-behind-the-counter, as easily and completely as she had been, before, one of the student community. Once, I accompanied her as she swiftly and confidently took a cardboard box full of rubbish to that special, secluded area in the market where refuse was emptied, and collected later by a truck. She was herself, and yet wholly transformed.

Strange place, Oxford, and strange discoveries one makes within it! Strange students' rooms, with their own, always slightly unfamiliar, dimensions. During that time when I was undecided between Shehnaz and Mandira, hurting them both, being hurt by both, confused as I had never been, I lived on the ground floor of the graduate building, and Sharma lived in the room just above mine; we had a floor and a ceiling in common. From the beginning, Shehnaz and I tried in various ways, in kind and unkind, in rational and irrational ways, to shake off each other; but Oxford is such a lonely place, such a small place, so few its streets and its landmarks, that those who have felt some affection for each other come together again and again. When I went missing (and sometimes I was with Mandira), Shehnaz would wait for me to return in Sharma's room. Coming back, I would hear that Shehnaz had been looking for me; going to her college, I would not find her there. For long periods of our relationship, if one were to add all these moments, we kept ourselves absent or hidden from each other. On one occasion, I remember, I had been out for several hours; she had come twice to my room and gone away. When she came for the third time, I was in Sharma's room, and we saw her from his window, coming down the road. As she rang the doorbell, entered, and then climbed up the stairs, Sharma said, 'Quick, hide in the cupboard!'; it was something he himself loved doing, a bad but endearing habit, surprising me by stepping into my closet when I was not there, and then coming out and taking me unawares. Guided by him, without a will of my own, I was led inside, to stand there among Sharma's shirts and trousers as he opened his door and asked Shehnaz in. Silent, hidden, I watched through the crack between two doors, which gave me a surprisingly wide vision as Shehnaz, dressed in churidar and kurta, sat on the armchair and asked in a puzzled way, 'What, is he out again?' and Sharma replied nonchalantly, 'No, no, he is here, he is somewhere here.' And yet, I did not, like Sharma, have the courage to emerge.

Twenty Three

Sohanlal was born in a kingdom in Rajasthan and, as a boy, he became a court dancer. There were times when he had to perform before the king, when his guru would take him and another boy to dance as Radha and Krishna at the court. When the dance was over, the audience would bow before the two children as if they *were* Radha and Krishna. That world, of gestures and wonder, existing in the wide, silent margins of the land, is gone now. All has been named and brought to consciousness, the colours, the words and their meanings, but Sohanlal is one of those few people who remember the darkness of what was there before, the old language and its life.

When we were alone, Sohanlal would show me the lanes of Brindaban, sitting on the floor with one leg crossed and the other knee raised, his bare feet visible but the rest of his legs covered by the white cotton cloth of his pyjamas, the upper part of his body in a silk kurta which descended and rested calmly upon his lap like a great handkerchief. His arm would be lifted at an angle that inclined towards his head. Brindaban appeared as he moved while singing the words in Avadhi that had been composed by Bindadeen Maharaj. Avadhi, an older version of Hindi, still spoken in the villages, is such a poetic language that its most common expressions can bring places and spirits before the eye, can stir love in the heart. Its discontinuous grammar and incomplete sentences are a product of the consciousness that existed before there was any difference between the past and present. When Sohanlal became Radha, his face would be turned away a little, in shyness and also in hurt at Krishna's transgressions, one eyebrow raised but the eyes averted. But when he was Krishna, he was the child Krishna, his lips smeared with curds and butter, or dancing upon the serpent's head, or swaying very lightly to his own music. Often, women would seek out his mother to complain of his mischief, and many times, when he stopped their path as they walked towards the River Yamuna, they had no choice but to threaten him and plead with Yasodha. All his excuses and alibis were known to her, but by the time he returned it had become evening and her heart was filled with love. The lies he said to her at that moment she pretended to believe.

When I hear the raag Maand, I think of my guru and his brother and Sohanlal, for it bears the characteristics, the stamp, and the life of their region. Their faces, their language, the colour of their skin, the cotton clothes they wear, are set and have their meaning against the same landscape. Each raag was once a folk-melody, a regional air sung, with tiny variations, to different words, by members of a community of families before its notes were ordered and systematised into the melodic progression called a raag. But when a Rajasthani sings Maand, or a Punjabi sings Sindhi Bhairavi, he returns to his homeland, which for him is a certain landscape influenced by seasons, a certain style of dressing and speaking, a web of interrelationships and festive occasions. Each region has its own grace-notes, its peculiar turns in singing, and there were some grace-notes I had to learn and relearn arduously which Sohanlal told me came naturally and without practise to the people of his land, from temple singers to young peasant boys. Maand was a raag which, when sung by my guru or Sohanlal, revealed its airy, skeletal frame, with holes and gaps in it, its unnameable, magical beginnings, and its spirit-like mobility in covering distances, in traversing scorched mountainsides, deserts, horizons, water, following back on the route of migrations that had led away from that country. The raags, woven together, are a history, a map, a calendar, of Northern India, they are territorial and temporal, they live and die with men, even though they seem to be timeless and exist outside them; they are evidence of the palimpsest-like texture of Northern India, with its many dyes and hues, its absence of written texts and its peculiar memory, so that no record of people like Sohanlal, or my guru and guru's father, exists unequivocally, or without rhythm and music.

Each raag has its time of day, a cluster of hours called 'prahar', or its season. Goud Sarang and Shudh Sarang are sung at midday, while Madhuvanti in late afternoon verging on twilight, Purvi and Shree from dusk to early evening, and in late evening, Abhogi Kanhra. Midday brings the smell of ripening jackfruit, the buzz and gleam of bluebottle flies, the fragrance of mango blossoms which, Tagore said, opens the doorways to heaven. The notes sa re ma re ma pa of Shudh Sarang, with the sharp and yearning ascent of the second ma, its resolution in pancham, define the bright inactivity of midday, its ablutions and rest, the peace of a household. Twilight cools the veranda; midday's boundary of protective shade separating household from street, inside from outside, is dissolved, the sad, flat rishab in conjunction with the sharp madhyam and pancham, the notes of Shree related to each other by dancing swoops and curves, calm the mind during the withdrawal of light. No raag is so pure that it does not remind one of another raag, that it is not, in some elementary way, a variation or version of a raag sung at some other time of day, or some other season. For instance, does not the heat and blaze of Shudh Sarang resemble, in its structure and shape, the watery gravity and plumbings of Megh? The seasons and hours have no absolute existence, but are defined by each other.

Twenty Four

In the last and hottest days of summer, Bombay waited for the rains to arrive. The earth hardened into brown Deccan bedrock, the black rocks by the Arabian Sea were warm if one touched them, people pulled curtains across the windows in the afternoon; it was a time of stupefying heat when reeds and grass grew long and leaned against walls, mango and jackfruit ripened, and flame-red gulmohurs lit the trees. The first drops of rain were a spray that moistened the cloth of one's shirt. This was the time when letters and newspapers arrived partially wet, the wet paper became soft, the parts of the newspaper it had rained upon darkened by a blue-grey shadow. For those who lived in houses like ours and owned a car, it was a season that brought relief; for the maidservants, sweepers, and part-time servants, who too, in a sense, 'lived' in Bombay, it was a time of trials and miracles, when one side of their roof collapsed and another side of their house blew away.

In August, in the last quarter of the monsoons, there would be a gathering, in memory of my guru's father's spiritual teacher, in a small temple in old Bombay, a community extravaganza that began early in the evening and continued to the dawn of the next day, as, one by one, musicians came and performed their piece and received my guru's family's disorganised hospitality and then left, while that family, with its grandfathers, daughters-in-law, and children, stayed wide awake through the night. My mother and I were invited to sing as well, and we took this performance seriously. So we set out in our Ambassador, with the tanpura resting on the front seat, and went down the drizzly roads of North Bombay, past eating-houses, local railway stations, old cinema halls, in search of the Ganesh temple at Matunga, which was our landmark. There, upon asking directions, the car turned into a lane, a shaded avenue of middle-class Marathi civility, where, in the houses, boys did their homework and young girls, their hair tied in a plait, studied harder than the boys and learned natya sangeet from their mothers, and, in the other room, the father-in-law, a widower, waited for dinner, while his son stood on the balcony in a vest and pyjamas. Through this lane we passed till noises were heard and lights were seen. All the family was there, in the courtyard adjoining the small temple, and already there was a singer performing inside, his

110

voice heard and serenely ignored as it came through a loudspeaker. The women – my guru's mother, his wife, Mohan's and Sohanlal's wives – sat together in a small room with no door, to enter which one had to take off one's sandals. Distant cousins, ne'er do well uncles in dhotis and turbans, irresponsible brothers-in-law who were fathers to several children, hung around in semi-joyous, semi-disgraced abeyance in the festive crowd, and were always available when an extra cymbal player or tanpura player was needed. Family snobberies, hierarchies, bonds, made themselves felt from the powerful, segregated clan of elderly women to the excited children in shiny clothes. This was my guru's world, a little Rajasthani village in Bombay.

This community would rematerialise in much the same way at funerals and weddings, and at the airport on the two occasions when my guru went to England. Then the traveller abroad was blessed by the elders, and nearly everyone was given a chance to hug and garland him, from close to seldom-seen relatives who reappeared at such moments to display family love and solidarity. This solidarity, which was a form of dependency, for the poorer relatives used this as an opportunity to ask favours of those who, like my guru, were doing better for themselves, became evident again, in all its formal comedy and transient but sincere show of love, during my guru's illness. I was then in Oxford; my parents were preparing to sell that flat in the suburbs and leave Bombay for ever. My mother described it to me later; the clan, enlarged now by concerned relatives who had come down from the villages for this special purpose, rallied around my guru and made every effort to hasten his death. Some of them came and stayed in his tiny flat; for them, it was a pilgrimage to see Bombay. A few years ago, my guru and his brother had sold their 'chawl' in King's Circle, and, with government loans, bought two flats, one for each brother, in Versova and Andheri. This, for them, had been like a liberation from an old and stifling way of life. Once, when my mother went to visit my guru in Versova during his illness – a recently developed area, with new buildings and roads alternating with patches of marshy land – she found the creation of a great lunch in progress, the women chopping spinach and boiling milk in the kitchen, the relatives moving about in the tiny space of the 'hall', careful not to step on the small shoals of children, the aroma of food spreading through the house, an anecdote being developed and an observation elaborated, while my guru lay on his side on the bed that was next to the front door, his head on the pillow, watching all this. In Bombay, where property is sold at thousands of rupees per square foot, each inch of space is magnified; a hall is called a hall, a bedroom a bedroom, though none of these rooms may be larger in size than a kitchen. The laughing Rajasthani women wore bright chiffon sarees, draped it over their heads, and kept a small part of their faces symbolically covered with the last remnant of a veil. In all that crowded commotion, medicines were given at the wrong time, or forgotten. The fabric of an ancient hospitality, irrelevant courtesies, meaningless gestures of goodwill, all-important in the creation of the decorum of that village-life – and they owned little else but that decorum – this was eternal, non-individual, it would go on; and, already, my guru was an outsider to it, he was leaving it behind. After he died, this life, as expected, continued cheerfully, divided from death only by a thin, transparent border; my guru's wife saw him in her dreams; sometimes he reassured her that he was happy 'over there'; at other times, he gave her sound financial advice: 'Eat chutney and chappati but don't sell the flat.' Influential government servants whose daughters or wives had been taught by my guru came forward to help his widow and children; helped her to set up a small, government retail shop that sold milk, peas, and meat. Then my guru stopped appearing in dreams.

Twenty Five

The old Calcutta airport, a dignified colonial bungalow with potted plants, is gone, but the 'new' domestic airport, now proxying as the international airport, stands and welcomes arriving passengers. Most of the travellers, coming or leaving, belong to Calcutta itself, Bengalis or Marwaris with children running from the bookshop at one end to the coffee-stall at the other. Outside, in the light, a crowd of boys and young men wait perpetually to greet the passengers as they emerge, to take their suitcases, to offer them taxis. You shoo them away; you try to ignore them; and then they have already forgotten you, they have found someone else, or are quarrelling playfully with each other. But one or two of the younger ones will reappear at the car-park and run with the car and see you off for the gift of a coin.

As a child, I used to come here with my parents for my holidays; but this time, returning from England, my parents were waiting for me outside the arrival area, my father and mother standing in the light, while passengers, pursued by those exuberant, sparrow-like local boys, passed before them, negotiating trolleys. Was it my imagination, or had some of Calcutta's black vapour darkened their complexions a shade? They looked as if they had been exposed to the sun, and seemed smaller as they stood there. But when I asked them, they said it might be because they had woken early in the morning; and here they were to receive me.

The drive homeward goes past a village scene, with huts, plantains, lakes, and malnourished but energetic children. Then, without hiatus, the city begins with a great drum-roll of traffic and one is in the midst of a marketplace of houses, tailors' and butchers' shops, billboards, and tramlines, bargaining for movement, haggling to go forward. Nothing has changed for the last twenty years. The Bengalis are like Irish families, except that they are small in height and the men have no access to drink, but the city is a mixture of officiousness and circumlocution that makes one despair. The air is awash with Marx and Trotsky; the airport, to which no international flight but Aeroflot and the Bangladesh Biman has been coming for years, is no gateway to fresh influences from abroad, but an interesting, if puzzling, building: and in Calcutta, nothing has happened after Marxism and modernism. In tea-shops and street corners, Bengali men, as ever, indulge in 'adda', a word that means both a pointless, pleasurable exchange of opinions and information, and the place or rendezvous in which it is conducted; if it were possible to say, for instance, of a certain kind of languorous conversation in England, 'I'm having a pub,' its quality might be approximately communicated in English.

And on the roads, one's neighbours are still Ambassadors, created by the Birlas from odds and ends – the body of a Morris Oxford and a tractor's engine – outnumbering by far any other car. Ours still has its old Bombay numberplate. On the Ambassador one finds perhaps the only doors that have to be slammed shut, with the maximum of force, without any intention of venting ill-temper, but as a perennial good-humoured habit as one gets in and gets out. Families that own them have had them for twenty years, half the duration of independence, in which time they have been repaired, repainted, sent to garages, reupholstered, and, when the owner is in straitened circumstances, left exposed to the elements. Every few years, the Birlas produce a new model at their factory, Mark III, Mark IV, which exactly replicates the previous one; for the Ambassador has remained faithful to the ideal that was perfected in the secure, organic era of the 'protected market', and, in its shape, still retains that philosophical look, that aura of being cut-off from the 'real' world: squat, conservative, and spacious.

Cruising downtown in it, one risks the bother of paying a tax to the municipal corporation if one parks it. The tax is collected by men who, sweating from running from car to car in the sun, slip a ticket under the wiper when you are away, and reappear punctually to collect the fee when you are back. Loafers and layabouts as described in the stories of Parashuram and Bibhutibhusan Bandhopadhaya, often charging you without giving you a ticket, they have taken up this job as human parking meters because they haven't found any other. The trouble they cause is brief, like a mosquito's sting, and subsides when one drives away.

When I arrived here in the summer, it was from an Oxford that had just gone through its annual dress-rehearsal and theatre of the exams. That was when Shehnaz finally put to use the notes she had made diligently over two years, when, after retching at her basin from nervousness, she would wear her black gown and set out early mornings through narrow cobbled lanes towards the Examination Schools, followed, and led, by other characters similarly dressed, some stepping out of the perfectly ordinary houses along the sides of the road. It was at this time that I began to realise that we were here in Oxford less as individuals than as students, attempting, in a touchingly innocent way, to complete a course and obtain a degree that would not only please us, but our parents, whoever and wherever they were. We were children sent here who, for a period of time till the exams began, behaved and felt like adults. Once the exams were finished the

117

childhood was over, the childhood of which even Shehnaz, Mandira, and I – the affection we felt for each other at our intersection of each other's life, and the loneliness of being in Oxford – were part.

A student fills the closet and shelves in his room with provisions that seem numerous when they are visible, but actually can be stuffed into one, at the most two suitcases. The student takes the coach to Heathrow; leaves by air; his books are packed in a crate and shipped after him, to travel out of the country upon the old sea-routes. The student's departure is deceptively fast, while his books' is slower, more weighted and material, and will reach his country only three months later. A few things are left behind in boxes in the college storeroom, or with friends, as if there were hope of returning in the future.

That summer in Calcutta, I sat and wrote a letter to America, to Shehnaz, and never posted it. Petty details and grievances, and a contradictory feeling of closeness, came to me as I was writing the letter. I took it with me to the General Post Office, a huge building on whose steps, all day, people ascend and descend dramatically, like the diminutive, busy men in the first black and white films. Inside, the Bengali male, dark, not more than five feet and five inches tall, hair carefully parted at the side, can be seen among pots of glue, or queueing up at one of the many windows where an employee sits portioning stamps, or having his letters weighed at a counter, and stamped with an archaic object that looks like a pestle. By evening, however, there is hardly anyone left, and the main room looks large and peaceful in the glow of fluorescent lights; a few employees working overtime sit behind counters, looking as porters on a provincial railway-station do after a train has left, the sense of departure, of a world beyond this one, having disappeared into the ordinariness of another evening and night. I had my letter weighed and stamped, and then decided not to send it. The thin, bespectacled clerk, in whose frail hand the ancient stamp looked so heavy and powerful, said irritably, 'You mean you want it back?' He explained to me the rules governing such procedures; he became, temporarily, the voice of the General Post Office; but I only saw before me a middle-aged Bengali whom, I felt vaguely, I already knew from a previous encounter. The more he sensed my frustration, the more he protracted his lecture on a higher logic that transcended personal ideas of reasonableness; and when he handed me the letter, he had me take it out of the envelope, which he tore thoroughly with his own hands.

Twenty Six

The two of them have been sleeping on the single bed, he against the wall, and she, lying on her back, next to him. Once, unable to bear her cramped position any more, she slipped off the bed on to the ground, her pillow with her. That was early in the morning. Now it is light. She gets up before him; she rummages among the shelves. She finds a jar of biscuits, and begins to eat them. When she peers through a crack in the curtains, she sees a hedge, and, barely visible above it, pinnacles and rooftops, the dreaming spires. Soon, outside the window, because it is summer, there will be visitors, a goose and a gander, one with pale brown feathers and the other with dark, translucent colours. Like the first tourists to discover a town, they explore the lawn together, though each, doggedly, keeps its distance from the other, maintaining a tangential, somewhat covert, relationship with the other's self-absorption, like the English couple, Henry and his wife, who are always separated by a few paces during their humdrum walks in *Monsieur Hulot's Holiday*. The days belong to these two, with their fussy, academic interests; they do not seem to be in the first flush of love, but in a period of retirement, discovering earthly wonders; and when a window is half opened, they quack acknowledgingly, rather than gratefully, at the thrower of crumbs, but never trouble themselves to look straight at a human face.

She wears her fluffy slippers, quietly opens the door, and goes to the bathroom so as not to disturb him; she solemnly washes her face, brushes her teeth, and combs her hair for almost a minute with her head bent sideways, as if thinking or remembering. Outside, she can hear other students making their first disconnected movements, the tentative noises, like those of a musical instrument being tuned, gradually accumulating and amplifying into a larger significance. She had never thought that she would give so much of herself to that boy still sleeping inside. He makes her angry, now that she loves his college and friends more than her own, and her heart is heavy with the distance she will have to travel. They were friends at first, they took walks, and then he wanted something more – and had she, too, wanted it? – and she found it more and more difficult to say no, to make him unhappy. And when he was unhappy . . . She makes herself a cup of coffee, and takes it back to the room. She will have to go

now, she says, but she will be back in the afternoon to help him pack. I'll go and start my own
packing now, she says. She wears her trousers and
shirt, which are lying on the chair in the shadow,
and picks up her things.

Stepping outside, into the clear June day,
she inhales the air and hugs herself, and, with
quick steps, crosses the road confidently, missing
two oncoming cars on either side. She feels
relieved, as if Oxford were new to her; as if nothing
had happened, and she had not known him, or
any of the other people. It takes two years of rainy
days, of human contact, to feel this moment of
freshness. This is what it should have been like in
the beginning, not the newcomer's worries and
desires, lived from moment to moment, the reck-
less craving for companionship and communi-
cation. She smiles and nods at the working men in
overalls and the scouts coming in; she is happiest
acknowledging people she has come to know by
sight. She begins to run towards her own college,
as the path curves, and students like herself come
out in twos and threes from the gate, quite blind
to her, and others go past singly and swiftly on
bicycles. She is still running down that path lined
with bicycles, where flowers have blossomed on
the hedges, and the canal flows on the other side.
A group of American academics wearing suits,
who are here to attend a conference, emerge,
unled, in an excited, bustling train from the doorway like schoolchildren who have lost sight of
their teacher. She is coming back to her college in

the morning, with its comforting hive-like rooms with large windows, in which students have woken up and parted their curtains, and their study-table, books, and table lamp are visible. She must say goodbye to her scout before she forgets, and to the boy who sits in at the porter's lodge in the evening, who used to once bravely dye his hair different colours; she must give them her address. Then, if she has time, she will walk down to the Bodleian to see if that book she had ordered before her exams has arrived; she still feels tempted, as if it were the treasured vestige of a discarded habit, to take a look at it. Will that leave her enough time to meet her tutor in North Oxford before lunch – that man whose ordinary, trustworthy name appears beneath the complicated and obscure titles of certain books she will put into her bag tonight, who used to write god-like but compassionate notes in an awesome hieroglyphic on the margins of her essays – and then come back in time to help him with his packing for the summer? The thought wearies her. The thought of parting, of never meeting again, of having to repeat to each other that they will see each other in December, of knowing that he will start again; Oxford wearies her. Just to study here, and go to the library, and walk up the stairs and come down again to have a sandwich at lunchtime; she could do that for ever. But it is never as simple as that. If she could choose, what would she choose? She is going back home to her parents and her wonderful, wisecracking sister, she will never mention it to them, and then she will get married. If she is married, she would like to have a baby in a year, it is something she has thought of, in a vague but intense way, for a long time. She will begin another life.

Twenty Seven

The first day I arrived in Oxford, it was raining, the fine, persistent, baby-like drizzle in which no one gets wet. Propelled and navigated by my suitcases, I found myself before a window in a centuries-old building which was now run, in a mood of chicanery and make-believe, as a fully operational shelter for scores of bright-spirited graduates in sweaters and jeans. I travelled then to my room in the modern annexe across the road, but returned each day, for food and letters, to that fairy-tale site, with its series of rooftops like witches' hats, which would disappear in a mist in January, its irregular flagstones outside the steps that had iron rings like knockers upon them (as if they opened onto secret underground entrances), and its mysterious employees who had ranks that set them apart as members of an ancient English sect – 'porter', 'steward', 'scout'. On my second day, I got a glimpse of Sharma in the dining room in the basement, dressed up like a provincial colonial, walking stiffly in a black suit I was never to see later, wearing it with that exact degree of painfulness that people do in the sweltering tropics, managing to look hot in it even in a cold country. His hair still possessed that neat and combed look imparted to it by an Indian barber, and he wore black-framed spectacles and a pencil-thin moustache, all of which constituted the cargo of his former life that he would lose accidentally, at one stroke, in a matter of weeks. But at that time, with a stern expression on his face, he resembled, with complete accuracy, the discomfited man facing the camera in his old passport photograph.

That was my second day. Even then, Shehnaz and Mandira were waiting to happen to me, for the rain and lack of sunlight had already entered me, from which I would create, inevitably, wisps of fantasy and desire that would later become flesh and bones and blood capable of breaking the heart, becoming one's own, and then, after a year, again changing into rain and grey light.

That year, I bought myself an Olympia typewriter, and tapped out, with one determined finger, essays and poems upon it. Word-processors and computers were then just coming into use, but I had no patience with the idea of leaving my room and crossing the road to the other building in order to familiarise myself with this new medium. I pretended to ignore it, and with one finger leaping blindly and instinctively from one key to the other, I laboriously but contentedly typed out my first essay on the Olympia. It was a unique object, with its arms fanning out and starting up individually when one touched a letter, a strange balance of mechanical harmony and obedience, an object that in the old days men used to call a 'machine', and feel unspeakably different from, a difference that produced both hostility and then later kinship. The computer is not a machine, but an equal in the marketplace, and one enters into no relationship with it, but surrenders to its strategic uses; but, in those days, I had not realised how indispensible it would become, and how its soft monochromatic hum would replace the hellish, Blakean, loud industrial noise of the typewriter.

Sharma, adept as he was at picking up new lifestyles and languages, embraced with generous openness, and without delay, both Wordstar and Wordperfect. With everything that was then new to him – except with meat, for he was an avowed vegetarian – he became friendly: computer-friendly, party-friendly, library-friendly, super-market-friendly. He was kitchen-friendly as well, and spent a good amount of time making food that emitted an aroma of spices that magnified the sense of what it meant to live in England. Demerara sugar, orange juice, nuts, a spiced lentil mixture he had bought at an Indian shop, and long-life milk were all assigned their places on the bookshelves and the window-sill in his room. 'Please have some nuts,' he would say in English;

or, in colloquial Hindi, offer me the lentils, scooping up a handful himself and tossing them mouthward. He used to be, then, in a state of constant excitement. When he was in a mood, or under pressure with work, his mind would always be flitting elsewhere, making his movements restless and his manner infuriatingly polite; one could see that he wasn't listening. But when he was at ease, he would be motherly and genuinely caring, and exude a strength that was strange in one who was so much more a foreigner to this land than I was. The matter of fact but buoyant way he began to cook the evening meal, the confidence with which he expressed himself in English, dropping articles and subverting grammar, made me think that my own sense of foreignness, of loneliness, was a luxury and an invention.

In those days, I could hardly experience England without being obtruded by what I had read about it in its literature and history. And even my compulsive nostalgia for home was half-imaginary. For Sharma, perception was a different thing; he discovered England afresh, and on him its impact was more direct, more immediately generous than it was on me; and yet, outwardly, he remained untouched. He had read Wordsworth and Shakespeare in India in Hindi translation; he loved *Macbeth*, especially the scene in which Dunsinane moves forward; he was not shy of picking up English customs or making English friends; and if he yearned for home, he did not mention it. Yet he did not exchange his persona for a new one, as many city-educated Indians do in England; he remained still and deep. The choices that existed in my world – between clinging to my Indianness, or letting it go, between being nostalgic or looking toward the future – did not exist in his. He was from a village in North India, and it was miraculous that he should be here in Oxford among other Indians of a different class, and it was the miracle of being in Oxford, of knowing Shehnaz, Mandira, of future meetings, incarnations, new faces, that I would become aware of when I was with him.

His room used to blaze with pictures of gods and goddesses. Each student inhabits at the beginning of the year a room with blank walls and empty shelves, and then makes of it what he will. Sharma stuck calendar pictures on the wall, in red, blue, orange, Kali biting her tongue, Parvati riding a tiger. They reminded me of roadside kitchens, of the backs of lorries, and the small radiant picture before the bus driver's seat. With their octopodal limbs, Kali's face faintly reminiscent of Hema Malini's, they were such good companions of the common man at home. Although they would have had no place in a middle-class house in Bombay, here in England, in Sharma's room, they existed for a while comfortingly and unironically.

By our second year, books occupied every inch of available space in the room. Sharma wished to understand the European mind, and nowhere so clearly and accessibly was Western culture contained as in books, and it was these books – Hawking's *A Brief History of Time*, *The Norton*

Anthology of English Literature, Collins' Thesaurus, *One Hundred Years of Solitude* – that were placed on Sharma's bookshelf. Many of them he did not read; but even buying a book at Blackwell's was a discovery; in one book was contained science; in another, meaning and pronunciation; in another, literature. Even novels, he found, had a peculiar wisdom to impart that he was not wholly unfamiliar with, having read the ancient Hindu epics; although as a child, studious and earnest, he had never read storybooks for being too trivial.

When, after midnight, we would settle down to a conversation, it would continue to the small hours of the morning, as, gradually, the graduate building became still around us, and Sharma told me of his childhood. His village was like a fiction; it had no electricity; it was not to be found on the map of India. He confessed this with a mixture of deprecation and pride. Such was the intensity of the dark in that village that when the landlords lit their petromax lamps a mile away the shadow of that light fell on the earthen walls of Sharma's house. His mother, whose photograph now hung in his room, was a frail woman of puritan fervour and great vision; his father was an idle, fun-loving dandy who liked nothing more than a gossip with the other men of the village. These two, for the most part, treated each other like distant relatives and led their own lives. Sharma and his older brother grew up in their mother's wings in a village which, with its vain and ignorant landlords, its huddled families, its canals, fields, and thunderstorms, was a little universe. Sharma travelled outward first by foot, to a school in a neighbouring town; then, years later, on a train, he arrived at the big city; and finally, by another train, he went to Delhi. During our conversations, I grew familiar with the shadowy, marginal figures – well-wishers, relatives, friends, villains, and oppressors – who all, without knowing it, became impartial co-ordinates in his determined but steady progress outward, away from them. As he spoke, I would smell chick-peas being roasted in their shells; I would wake up one morning to find the ceiling in an uncle's room had collapsed around him, barely disturbing his sleep; I would be full of revolutionary rhetoric when officials rigged the local elections; I would dress as Hanuman the monkey on a festival; I would travel sitting on the floor of a third-class train compartment to Lucknow; I would hear the roar of motorcycles and taste dust as the landlord's sons arrived at the earthen house. When Sharma spoke, reality and fancy, my past and his, became reordered in new proportions.

He was a sensitive person. A memory, a poem, or a song could move him so much that sometimes a tear, large and sticky, would roll out from a corner of his eye when he was recounting it to me. He would either wipe it away with a quick, self-conscious movement, or dab his eye patiently with his handkerchief. There were occasions when I would say something that would offend him, and we would not speak to each other for hours, or even the whole day.

131

One evening, he came down to my room in his shorts, with a cup of coffee in his hand. This was not unusual; it meant that we were going to be engaged in a conversation which would take us to the realms of autobiography, or throw us into an abstract discussion on religion, or make us pause over the nuances of literary experience. His face was grave, like one who has something important to communicate – perhaps a piece of bad news. 'I am very happy,' he said solemnly, 'that you are studying Lawrence.' I gave this remark its due weight. 'Last night, in my room, I read "Snake". It is beautiful,' he said. 'Then I read "Ship of Death". It's *great* poem, it is very rich. But I cannot decide between the two.'

Taking out, without further digression, my copy of the *Complete Poems*, he read out loud and clear, as if he were singing:

Have you built your ship of death, O have you?
O build your ship of death, for you will need it.

Coming next to me, he pointed out these lines, asking me, quite seriously, if I had read them:

A little ship, with oars and food
and little dishes, and all accoutrements
fitting and ready for the departing soul . . .

'Of course you must have,' he conceded apologetically. 'I believe you must have read every word by Lawrence.'

Each time these lines bring to me the idea of a seascape, and sometimes other conflicting pictures, like the memory of daal and sweet-potatoes being ground and mashed all day in the kitchen, then patted, shaped, and fried into pithhas, and left overnight in syrup; my mother choosing the brownest one for me, and the little less perfect one for my father.